THE
ULTIMATE
CHRISTMAS
CRACKER

THE
ULTIMATE
CHRISTMAS
CRACKER

JOHN JULIUS
NORWICH

Introduction by Julian Fellowes

JOHN MURRAY

This selection first published in Great Britain in 2019 by John Murray (Publishers)
An Hachette UK company

3

Copyright in the selection and editorial matter
© The Estate of John Julius Norwich 1970–2019
Introduction © Julian Fellowes 2019
Introduction to the Unfinished Christmas Cracker © Artemis Cooper 2019

A CIP catalogue record for this title is available from the British Library

Hardback ISBN 978-1-529-32490-7
eBook ISBN 978-1-529-32491-4

Text design by Janette Revill

Typeset in Fournier MT by Hewer Text UK Ltd, Edinburgh
Printed and bound in Great Britain by Clays Ltd, Elcograf S.p.A.

John Murray policy is to use papers that are natural, renewable and
recyclable products and made from wood grown in sustainable forests.
The logging and manufacturing processes are expected to conform
to the environmental regulations of the country of origin.

John Murray (Publishers)
Carmelite House
50 Victoria Embankment
London EC4Y 0DZ

www.johnmurraypress.co.uk

Contents

Introduction by Julian Fellowes   vii

From Still More Christmas Crackers, 1990–1999   1

1970–1979   5

1980–1989   35

1990–1999   63

2000–2009   87

2010–2018   121

2019   191

Acknowledgements   206

Index   208

Introduction by Julian Fellowes

In my business, if you get anywhere at all, you are often asked about the influences that guided you. Who was your inspiration? And normally one just fudges an answer and hopes it isn't too silly. But I am happy to declare that John Julius was a tremendous influence on me, from the moment we met more than thirty-five years ago. This was partly because of his achievements which were already considerable, but mainly because of the man he was. He wore his success so lightly, so gracefully; he was never patronising, or self-important, or pompous. And I remember thinking: if I am ever successful at all, this is the way to do it.

We were introduced by a mutual friend, Micky Nevill, and we became pals more or less at once – partly because we were almost the only people we knew who could exchange historical minutiae. He rapidly became a kind of magic man to me, a fairy godfather providing sudden and unexpected treats. 'Are you free for lunch?' And there we would be, in an unknown restaurant, north of the park, devouring delicious food and debating whether Madame de Pompadour had a sense of irony. Or sometimes I would be included in a dinner at Blomfield Road, where he and Mollie invariably hosted the most fascinating groups of people.

He telephoned me on my wedding day in 1990, when I was in the bath. For some reason I forget, they couldn't come to the wedding itself, and he had clearly forgotten the significance of the date, so we chatted on in our usual way – Was Caspar Hauser really the Grand Duke of Baden? Were we right to let the Italian monarchy fall in 1946? – until I said, 'John Julius, I'm loving this but the fact is, I'm getting married in a few minutes and I really feel I ought to concentrate on that.'

'Good God,' he said. 'So you are. Where are you going for your honeymoon?'

'The Gritti in Venice.'

'Good choice.'

'I hope so, although I'm rather worried about the food.' John Julius knew that I felt the Austrian occupation of the city in the nineteenth century had cast a long shadow over Venetian cuisine.

'You're a fool. You just don't know where to go.'

Anyway, the next day Emma and I arrived at the Gritti and there was a message from John Julius at reception, saying that he would be flying in on Thursday and he would take us out for dinner. Sure enough he arrived and whisked us off for a wonderful dinner in a wonderful restaurant. The John Julius Effect.

A few years later he called early one morning. 'What do you know about Carlo Goldoni?'

'Who?'

'Carlo Goldoni. Eighteenth-century playwright. *The Servant of Two Masters*. What do you know about him?'

'Absolutely nothing.'

'Well, this is the point. Every year I give a lecture – you have to give it twice – for Save Venice, and this year I was due to have spoken about Goldoni. But something's come up and I can't go, so I've told them you are the greatest expert on Goldoni in England and, since I can't do it, they must offer it to you. You'll have a marvellous time. They put you up and you visit all these private palaces. You'll love it.'

I said, 'It sounds a terrific plan, but it has a flaw. I don't know a bleeding thing about Goldoni.'

'You can read, can't you?'

I replied that I could. 'Well, then. If you can read, you can give a lecture.' And this, of course, was quintessential John Julius, always one to make light of his gifts. If he could do it, anyone could do it. Except that they couldn't. At any rate, not nearly as well as he. But there was another result from this approach: it made the impossible seem possible. And, sure enough, a few weeks later I found myself in Venice, giving two lectures on Goldoni, while Emma and I had a blissful ten days at the Monaco, visiting secret palaces and admiring the villas on the Brenta.

One of the great privileges of being a friend of John Julius was to find oneself on the receiving list of the famous Christmas Cracker booklets which were sent out, once a year, as a kind of super-Christmas-card. I learned later that he had fallen into the habit of collecting short passages that made him laugh quite early in his adult life. These could come from anywhere.

Having started with various crushed and crumpled notebooks, he took to keeping these entries in a rather smart book, given by his mother Lady Diana Cooper, when he was living in Beirut in 1957. In those days of refuelling aeroplanes for long journeys, Beirut was often a city where people stayed a night before continuing their journey east, and so Lady Diana thought her son and his wife would be doing a great deal of entertaining. Unfortunately, this was not the case but the book rapidly filled up – soon he needed more. In 1970 he had the idea of getting a selection of these entries published, mostly for distribution to his friends and partly to sell. Much to his surprise the Christmas Cracker proved a great success from the start and became an annual event. John Julius went on to create forty-nine Crackers, each one a superb collection that ranged from the sublime to the ridiculous (mostly the ridiculous), with his warm, wry sense of the absurdity of human pretension colouring all of them. I treasure these little booklets and have kept them, safely stored, to this day. It was a sort of annual reminder of why we all loved him.

I managed to attend his last book launch. It was quite a struggle to get there, but somehow I sensed I would regret it if I didn't. The book, *France: A History – From Gaul to de Gaulle*, is astonishing. A single volume, and not a very fat one, which tells you everything you could ever need to know about the history of France from Roman times to the Second World War, and it reads like a thriller. Anyway, on that evening John Julius was on top form, speaking from the gallery at Daunt's, as self-deprecating and funny as ever. Afterwards I fought through his crowd of admirers, conscious that I wanted to say something meaningful to him. I had a suspicion that we might not meet again and it seemed important that I should somehow tell him what a tremendous figure he had been in my life. But, alas, I am English and an Englishman does not normally manage these matters very well. So we blathered away for a bit, saying nothing of any great worth, and then his fans closed in and I went home. But I am glad I was there, as it allows me to testify today that the man I knew, humorous, clever, modest, charming, graceful . . . he was that man to the very last.

Julian Fellowes
April 2019

Look, what thy memory cannot contain,
Commit to these waste blanks, and thou shalt find
Those children nursed, deliver'd from thy brain,
To take a new acquaintance of thy mind.

Shakespeare, Sonnet 77

From Still More Christmas Crackers, 1990–1999

For the benefit of newcomers, I should explain that when I was living in Beirut in the late 1950s my mother gave me a beautiful album, bound in dark-blue Nigerian goatskin, which she intended to be used as a visitors' book. Unfortunately, within days of the volume's arrival, civil war broke out; the Lebanese government declared a curfew and for several months thereafter we had no visitors at all. There was, on the other hand, plenty of time for reading; and the little notebook in which I had been in the habit of noting down short passages that had, for one reason or another, caught my fancy was fast filling up. One evening, therefore, when I had nothing better to do, I decided to copy them all into my still virgin album.

Then something remarkable happened. Instead of a heterogeneous pile of literary jottings, I suddenly real-ised that I had a proper commonplace book, something to be cultivated and nurtured and treasured, and to which the luxuriously tooled and gilded binding seemed to confer a wholly unexpected distinction. Some five years later that first album was full and I ordered another, in exactly the same format but this time in dark red. This was followed in due course by another, and another, with the colour changing each time . . .

But commonplace collections, like every other kind, are no fun if they are not shared; and in the autumn of 1970 I decided to have a little booklet printed containing a couple of dozen of my choicest items, and to send it round to my friends as a sort of glorified Christmas card. Production costs were modest in those days, and even these, I thought, might be recovered if I were to order a hundred or so extra copies and persuade one or two friendly booksellers to dispose of them as best they could.

The edition disappeared gratifyingly quickly, and so the following year I produced another – increasing my print order, in a burst of reckless optimism from two hundred to three. That too sold out; and it was thus that the uncertain seedling became a moderately hardy annual, and I now find myself introducing the combined harvest of its third decade.

Previously I listed what seemed to me the advantages of a commonplace collection such as mine. 'First of all,' I pointed out, 'it costs literally nothing; nicely bound volumes are useful for providing the initial impetus and for creating the sense of pride that every collector must develop to keep him going, but they are in no way essential. Secondly, being totally divorced from monetary wealth, it knows no restrictions of size or scope, accepting only those limitations which the collector himself decides to impose; it follows that no other form of collection can so fully reflect his taste and personality. Thirdly, he is on his own, far away from the world of catalogues and sale-rooms, experts and dealers. Indeed, one of the first lessons he learns is never to go out looking for anything; he is very unlikely to find it if he does, and the very act of searching seems in some curious way to blunt the antennae. If he can only keep these sharp, there is no telling where and when he will make his next *trouvaille*. He may not even need to wait until he next picks up a book; a chance remark, a letter from a friend, an opera programme, an advertisement, the instruction book for a new washing machine, a visit to a country church, a notice in a hotel room or railway station – any of these things, or a thousand others, can reveal the unexpected nugget of pure gold.'

The mix is everything. The grave must lie down with the gay, the poetry with the prose, the cynical with the sad; and it is not always easy to make them do so.

John Julius Norwich
July 2000

1970–1979

My mother taught me to read with the aid of a splendid little volume called Reading Without Tears, or a Pleasant Mode of Learning to Read, by the Author of 'Peep of Day', &c. *It was published in 1861 and has been reprinted. Where I was concerned, it did its job swiftly and, as promised, painlessly; but the other day I looked through it again, and wondered. Here are two extracts:*

What is the mat-ter with the lit-tle boy?

He has ta-ken poi-son. He saw a cup of poi-son on the shelf. He said, 'This seems sweet stuff.' So he drank it.

Why did he take it with-out leave?

Can the doc-tor cure him? Will the poi-son des-troy him? He must die. The poi-son has des-troyed him.

Wil-li-am climb-ed up-stairs to the top of the house, and went to the gun-pow-der clos-et. He fil-led the can-is-ter. Why did he not go down-stairs quickly? It came into his fool-ish mind, 'I will go in-to the nur-se-ry and fright-en my lit-tle bro-thers and sis-ters.'

It was his de-light to fright-en the chil-dren. How un-kind! He found them a-lone with-out a nurse. So he was a-ble to play tricks. He throws a lit-tle gun-pow-der in-to the fire. And what hap-pens? The flames dart out and catch the pow-der in the can-is-ter. It is blown up with a loud noise. The chil-dren are thrown down, they are in flames. The win-dows are bro-ken. The house is sha-ken.

Mis-ter Mor-ley rush-es up-stairs. What a sight! All his chil-dren ly-ing on the floor burn-ing. The ser-vants help to quench the flames. They go for a cab to take the chil-dren to the hos-pit-al. The doc-tor says, 'The chil-dren are blind, they will soon die.'

~

A poem by Thomas Moore that deserves, I think, to be better known as we rocket ourselves into the space age:

They may rail at this life – from the time I began it
I found it a life full of kindness and bliss;
And, until they can show me some happier planet,
More social and bright, I'll content me with this.
As long as the world has such lips and such eyes
As before me this moment enraptured I see,
They may say what they will of their orbs in the skies,
But this earth is the planet for you, love, and me.

In Mercury's star, where each minute can bring them
New sunshine and wit from the fountain on high,

Though the nymphs may have livelier poets to sing
    them,
They've none, even there, more enamour'd than I.
And, as long as this harp can be waken'd to love
And that eye its divine inspiration shall be,
They may talk as they will of their Edens above,
But this earth is the planet for you, love, and me.

In that star of the west, by whose shadowy splendour,
At twilight so often we've roam'd through the dew,
There are maidens, perhaps, who have bosoms as
    tender,
And look, in their twilights, as lovely as you.
But though they were even more bright than the queen
Of that Isle they inhabit in heaven's blue sea,
As I never those fair young celestials have seen,
Why – this earth is the planet for you, love, and me.

As for those chilly orbs on the verge of creation,
Where sunshine and smiles must be equally rare,
Did they want a supply of cold hearts for that station,
Heaven knows, we have plenty on earth we could spare.
Oh! think what a world we should have of it here,
If the haters of peace, of affection and glee,
Were to fly up to Saturn's comfortless sphere,
And leave earth to such spirits as you, love, and me.

Useful palindromes:

What other words would spring to the lips when breaking the news of the death of a prize herd of cattle, suddenly smitten with infective epilepsy?

Stiff, O dairyman! In a myriad of fits!

Dr Barnardo making out the menus:

Desserts I desire not,
so long no lost one rise distressed.

Finally, the rebuke of the high-principled lady to her rich Norman lover:

Diamond light, Odo, doth gild no maid.

~

One of the most unusual coronations in history must have been that of the Persian King Shapur II in AD 309. Here is Gibbon on the subject.

The wife of Hormouz remained pregnant at the time of her husband's death, and the uncertainty of the sex, as well as of the event, excited the ambitious hopes of the princes of the house of Sassan. The apprehensions of civil war were at length removed by the positive assurance of the Magi that the widow of Hormouz had conceived, and would safely produce a son. Obedient to the voice of superstition, the Persians prepared, without delay, the ceremony of his coronation. A royal bed, on which the queen lay in state, was exhibited in the midst of the palace, the diadem was placed on the spot which might be supposed to conceal the future heir of Artaxerxes, and the prostrate satraps adored the majesty of their invisible and insensible sovereign.

~

Some time ago I discovered, tucked inside my father's copy of Through the Looking-Glass, *an autographed letter from the author. It is obviously addressed – despite the internal evidence ostensibly to the contrary – to a little girl. It strikes me as wonderfully characteristic – no one else could possibly have written it – but isn't it a bit sinister as well?*

March 30, 1861.
Ch. Ch. Oxford.

My dear Kathleen,

I promised once, if you remember, to send you one of these little penknives on your next birthday, and I hope this will arrive in time. I send it with my wishes for your good health, and many happy returns of your 72nd birthday. (Do not be surprised at my knowing your age: Henrietta told me, or I should never have guessed it, since you certainly do not look so old.) I hope you will find this knife as good as the one which you told me you lost about forty years ago.

I will tell you a few ways in which you will find it useful. First, you should cut your meat at dinner with it: in this way you will be safe from eating too much, and so making yourself ill. If you find that when the others have finished you have only had one mouthful, do not be vexed about it but say to yourself '*I will eat quicker tomorrow*.' Then, when you go for a walk, if you hadn't this knife you might be in danger of tiring yourself by walking too far – but now, by simply making a rule always to *cut your name on every tree you come to*, I am sure you will never go far enough to do yourself any harm. Besides this, whenever you wish to punish your brothers, their hands and faces (particularly the end of the nose); you will find it gives a good deal of pain if you run it in hard enough.

No doubt you will find out many other ways in which this knife will be useful, and I hope to hear that you like it, and always use it in the ways which I have mentioned. If you think of writing (and mind you don't sign yourself 'K' again – I know no young lady of *that*

name), my direction will be C. L. Dodgson Esq.,
J. Hunt Esq., Ore House, near Hastings till the 6th
of April, and after that Ch. Ch. Oxford. So, my dear
Kathleen, I remain

Your affte. friend
Charles L. Dodgson

~

I have just discovered what a pennill *is. It is a traditional
Welsh form of improvised verse, normally sung to a harp
accompaniment. The plural is* pennillion – *a nice plural.
This particular example, translated by Geoffrey Grigson,
dates from the seventeenth century:*

> What happiness you gave to me
> Underneath this graveyard tree
> When in my embraces wound,
> Dear heart, you lay above the ground.

*The same thought, if somewhat differently expressed, can be
found in James Thurber's glorious parody of those novels
about the Deep South like* Tobacco Road *or* God's Little
Acre. *It is called* Bateman Comes Home *and begins:*

Old Nate Birge sat on the rusted wreck of an ancient sewing-machine, in front of Hell Fire, which is what his shack was known as among the neighbors and to the police. He was chewing on a splinter of wood and watching the moon come up lazily out of the old cemetery in which nine of his daughters were lying, only two of whom were dead.

~

Adam, a brown old vulture in the rain,
Shivered below his wind-whipped olive-trees;
Huddling sharp chin on scarred and scraggy knees,
He moaned and mumbled to his darkening brain;
'He was the grandest of them all – was Cain!
'A lion laired in the hills, that none could tire;
'Swift as a stag; a stallion of the plain,
'Hungry and fierce with deeds of huge desire.'

Grimly he thought of Abel, soft and fair –
A lover with disaster in his face,
And scarlet blossom twisted in bright hair.
'Afraid to fight; was murder more disgrace? . . .
'God always hated Cain . . .' He bowed his head –
The gaunt wild man whose lovely sons were dead.

Siegfried Sassoon, 'Ancient History'

14

It is interesting to compare that sonnet by Sassoon with the following lines by Wilfred Owen. Both poets are haunted by the same theme — the carnage of the First World War in which they were both fighting — and both have found their inspiration in the Old Testament. But Owen goes deeper.

So Abram rose, and clave the wood, and went,
And took the fire with him, and a knife.
And as they sojourned both of them together,
Isaac the first-born spake and said, My Father,
Behold the preparations, fire and iron,
But where the lamb for this burnt-offering?
Then Abram bound the lad with belts and straps,
And builded parapets and trenches there,
And stretched forth the knife to slay his son.
When lo! an angel called him out of heaven,
Saying, Lay not thy hand upon the lad,
Neither do anything to him. Behold,
A ram, caught in a thicket by its horns;
Offer the Ram of Pride instead of him.

But the old man would not so, but slew his son —
And half the seed of Europe, one by one.

'The Parable of the Old Man and the Young'

Horace Walpole describes the funeral of George II in 1760:

When we came to the chapel of Henry the Seventh, all solemnity and decorum ceased; no order was observed, people sat or stood where they could or would; the yeomen of the guard were crying out for help, oppressed by the immense weight of the coffin; the Bishop read sadly, and blundered in the prayers; the fine chapter, *Man that is born of a Woman*, was chanted, not read; and the anthem, besides being immeasurably tedious, would have served as well for a nuptial. The real serious part was the figure of the Duke of Cumberland, heightened by a thousand melancholy circumstances. He had a dark brown adonis, and a cloak of black cloth, with a train of five yards. Attending the funeral of a father could not be pleasant: his face bloated and distorted with his late paralytic stroke, which has affected, too, one of his eyes, his leg extremely bad, yet forced to stand upon it near two hours, and placed over the mouth of the vault, into which, in all probability, he must himself so soon descend; think how unpleasant a situation! He bore it all with a firm and unaffected countenance. This grave scene was fully contrasted by the burlesque Duke of Newcastle. He fell into a fit of crying the moment he came into the chapel, and flung himself back in a stall, the Archbishop hovering over him with a smelling-bottle; but in two minutes his curiosity got the better of his hypocrisy, and he ran about the chapel with his glass to spy who was or was not there, spying with one hand, and mopping his eyes with the other. Then returned the fear of catching cold; and the Duke of Cumberland, who was sinking with heat, felt himself weighed down, and turning round, found it was the Duke of Newcastle standing upon his train, to avoid the chill of the marble.

Here, by contrast, is Benjamin Robert Haydon at the coronation of George IV on 19 July 1821:

The appearance of a monarch has something in it like the rising of a sun. There are indications which announce the luminary's approach; a streak of light – the tipping of a cloud – the singing of the lark – the brilliance of the sky, till the cloud edges get brighter and brighter, and he rides majestically in the heavens. So with a king's advance. A whisper of mystery turns all eyes to the throne. Suddenly two or three rise; others fall back; some talk, direct, hurry, stand still, or disappear. Then three or four of high rank appear from behind the throne; an interval is left; the crowds scarce breathe. Something rustles, and a being buried in satin, feathers, and diamonds rolls gracefully into his seat. The room rises with a sort of feathered, silken thunder.

If only Haydon could have painted as well as he wrote . . .

As a change from palindromes, try holorhymes — whole lines which have the same sound but different meanings. For some reason, they seem to go better in French. Louise de Vilmorin gave me two beautiful ones:

Étonnamment monotone et lasse
Est ton âme en mon automne, hélas!

and

Gall, amant de la reine, alla tour magnanime,
Gallament de l'arène à la Tour Magne, à Nîmes.

This second one is by Victor Hugo. Some time ago an entrant in a New Statesman competition made a bold stab at a translation. I noted it, but idiotically failed to note the author. If he sees this, I hope he will forgive me.

Gall, doll-lover, 'ghost' to royalty at right hour,
Galled all over, goes to royal tea at Rye Tower.

Here is another admirable one by Victor Hugo:

O! fragiles Hébreux! Allez, Rébecca, tombe!
Offre à Gilles zèbres, oeufs; à l'Erèbe, hécatombe!

Finally, and shortest of all, there is the poem about Zeus when metamorphosed as a swan:

Léda
L'aida

~

In the gallery of St Mary's Church, Paddington Green, now superbly restored, there is a memorial plaque which reads:

Near this Place lie the Remains of
John Christian Backhouse
First born Son of
John and Catherine Backhouse
Of the parish of St. Margaret, Westminster.
He was a Child of Exiguous Beauty of Form
and he had a Precociousness of Intellect
of a Character probably Unparalleled

. . .

He died on the 12th of May 1817
aged only Nine Months and 19 Days.

~

Many years ago, having lunch at Chantilly, Paddy Leigh Fermor and I were talking about how all Englishmen hated being seen to cry. Then and there we improvised a sonnet, each contributing alternate lines across the table. The whole thing was very light-hearted and took ten minutes at the most; but as I read it nearly a quarter of a century later it seems to me to have come out rather better than might have been expected. The odd-numbered lines are mine, the even his.

When Arnold mopped the English eye for good,
    And arid cheeks by ne'er a tear were furrowed,
Where each Rugbeian from the Romans borrowed
    The art of 'must' and 'can' from 'would' or 'should';
When to young England Cato's courage stood
Firm o'er the isle where Saxon sows had farrowed,
And where Epicurean pathways narrowed
    Into the Stoic porch of hardihood;

Drought was thy portion, Albion! Great revival!
    With handkerchief divorced at last from cane,
When hardened bums bespoke our isle's survival
    And all the softness mounted to the brain.
        Now tears are dried – but Arnold's shade still searches
        Through groves of golden rods and silver birches.

Two thoughts about pictures. First, by Kuo Hsi, a painter of the Sung period, born about AD *1020.*

To learn to draw a flower it is best to place a blossoming plant in a deep hollow in the ground and to look upon it. Then all its qualities may be grasped. To learn to draw a bamboo, take a branch and cast its shadow upon a white wall on a moonlight night; then its true outline can be obtained. To learn to paint a landscape, too, the method is the same. An artist should identify himself with the landscape and watch it until its significance is revealed to him.

Second, by Sir Thomas Browne in Religio Medici*:*

I can look for a whole day with delight upon a handsome picture, though it be but of an horse.

~

Lewis Carroll's 'Jabberwocky' is too well known to be included in a Cracker, *but this translation deserves to be remembered. It first appeared in the* New Yorker *on 10 January 1931:*

Le Jaseroque

Il brilgue: les tôves lubricilleux
Se gyrent en vrillant dans le guave,
Enmîmés sont les gougebosqueux,
Et le mômerade horsgrave.

'Garde-toi du Jaseroque, mon fils!
La gueule qui mord; la griffe qui prend!
Garde-toi de l'oiseau Jube, évite
Le frumieux Band-à-Prend!'

Son glaive vorpal en main, il va
T-à la recherche du fauve manscant;
Puis, arrivé à l'arbre Té-Té,
Il y reste, réfléchissant.

Pendant qu'il pense, tout uffusé,
Le Jaseroque, à l'oeil flambant,
Vient sibilant par le bois tullegeais,
Et burbule en venant.

Un deux, un deux, par le milieu
La glaive vorpal fait pat-à-pan!
La bête défaite, avec sa tête,
Il rentre gallomphant.

'As-tu tué le Jaseroque?
Viens à mon Coeur, fils rayonnais!

Ô Jour frabjeais! Calleau! Callai!'
Il cortule dans sa joie.

Il brilgue: les tôves lubricilleux
Se gyrent en vrillant dans le guave,
Enmîmés sont les gougebosqueux,
Et le mômerade horsgrave.

Frank L. Warrin Jr

Now here by contrast is a German rendering. It is by Dr Robert Scott, Master of Balliol and afterwards Dean of Rochester, who collaborated with Dean Liddell of Christ Church – Alice's father – on the great Greek Lexicon. Martin Gardner writes that 'it first appeared in an article, "The Jabberwock traced to its True Source", in Macmillan's Magazine, February 1872. Using the pseudonym of Thomas Chatterton, Scott tells of attending a seance at which the spirit of one Hermann von Schwindel insists that Carroll's poem is simply an English translation of the following old German ballad':

Der Jammerwoch

Es brillig war. Die schlichten Toven
   Wirrten und wimmelten im Waben;
Und allermümsige Burggoven
   Die mohmen Räth' ausgraben.

'Bewahre doch vor Jammerwoch!
    Die Zähne knirschen, Krallen kratzen!
Bewahr' vor Jubjub-Vogel, vor
    Frumiösen Banderschnätzchen!'

Er griff sein vorpals Schwertchen zu,
    Er suchte lang das manchsam' Ding;
Dann, stehend unten Tumtumbaum,
    Er anzudenken fing.

Als stand er tief in Andacht auf,
    Des Jammerwochens Augenfeuer
Durch tulgen Wald mit Wiffel kam
    Ein Burbelnd ungeheuer!

Eins, zwei! Eins, zwei! Und durch und durch
    Sein vorpals Schwert zerschnifferschnück!
Da blieb es todt! Erk, Kopf in Hand,
    Geläumfig zog zurück.

'Und schlugst du ja den Jammerwoch?
    Umarme mich, mein böhm'sches Kind!
O Freudentag! O Hallooschlag!'
    Er chortelt frohgesinnt.

Es brillig war. Die schlichten Toven
    Wirrten und wimmelten im Waben;
Und allermümsige Burggoven
    Die mohmen Räth' ausgraben.

Gilbert White, author of The Natural History and Antiquities of Selborne, *kept his journal for a quarter of a century, from 1768 to 1793 when he died. No literary work has ever recorded more precisely, more sensitively and yet with less pretension, the changing face of the countryside with the passing of the seasons. Most of the individual items are in themselves unmemorable – it is the cumulative effect that counts – but occasionally we are pulled up short:*

4 December 1770
Most owls seem to hoot exactly in B flat according to several pitch-pipes used in tuning of harpsichords, and as strictly at concert pitch.

8 February 1782
Venus *shadows* very strongly, showing the bars of the windows on the floors and walls.

The first of these entries brought a most serendipitous contribution from Antony Head, quoting Professor Howard Evans of Fort Collins, Colorado:

Even the simple wing sounds of midges and mosquitoes play a role in bringing the sexes together. In this case it is the female that attracts the male by the hum of her wings, a fact quickly apparent to singers who hit a G in the vicinity of a swarm and end up with a mouthful of male mosquitoes.

In the late Maurice Bowra's Memories, *he records a letter written to Penelope Betjeman by the Vicar of Baulking:*

Baulking Vicarage

My dear Penelope,

I have been thinking over the question of the playing of the harmonium on Sunday evenings here and have reached the conclusion that I must now take it over myself.

I am very grateful to you for doing it for so long and hate to have to ask you to give it up, but, to put it plainly, your playing has got worse and worse and the disaccord between the harmonium and the congregation is becoming destructive of devotion. People are not very sensitive here, but even some of them have begun to complain, and they are not usually given to doing that. I do not like writing this, but I think you will understand that it is my business to see that divine worship is as perfect as it can be made. Perhaps the crankiness of the instrument has something to do with the trouble. I think it does require a careful and experienced player to deal with it.

Thank you ever so much for stepping so generously into the breach when Sibyl was ill; it was the greatest possible help to me and your results were noticeably better then than now.

Yours ever,
F. P. Harton

Lord Byron's dog, Boatswain, was buried in the gardens of Newstead Abbey. His epitaph, which was once attributed to Byron himself but which we now know to have been written by Hobhouse, runs as follows:

Near this spot are deposited the remains of one who possessed Beauty without Vanity, Strength without Insolence, Courage without Ferocity, and all the Virtues of Man without his Vices. This praise, which would be unmeaning Flattery, if inscribed over human ashes, is but a just Tribute to the Memory of BOATSWAIN, a Dog.

My next favourite animal epitaph is that of Copenhagen, described on his tombstone as 'the charger ridden by the Duke of Wellington the entire day, at the Battle of Waterloo'. He was born in 1808 and died, after long years of honourable retirement, in 1836 at Stratfield Saye.

God's humbler instrument, though meaner clay,
Should share the glory of that glorious day.

~

Long ago, reading Garrett Mattingly's The Defeat of the Spanish Armada, *I came across the following sentence about Dr – later Cardinal – William Allen:*

Since he had left England William Allen had thoroughly learned, as another exile had learned before him, how steep the stairs are going up and down in strangers' houses, how bitter-salt the bread that exiles eat.

The extraordinary thing was that in those days I had no idea that the source was Dante, and that the images of the salty bread and the steep stairs were well known throughout the world. What Dante actually wrote, in Canto XVII of the Paradiso, *was:*

> Tu proverai si come sa di sale
> Lo pane altrui, e come è duro calle
> Lo scendere e 'l salir per l'altrui scale.

More recently, Mr David Rose of County Cork has drawn my attention to two other literary echoes of the same theme. The first is a quatrain from a poem called 'Famous Exiles', by H. W. Nevinson:

> And Dante up and down another's stairs,
> Abhorrent as the craggy depths of Hell,
> In exile climbed, though Rome's Imperial Care
> Wrenched at his heart that was love's citadel.

The second is part of an occasional poem written in a visitors' book by J. L. Motley, and quoted in Henry Chaplin: A Memoir, *by Lady Londonderry:*

> Bitter the bread –
> So Dante said –
> One eats at strangers' banquets,
> And ill he fares
> Who goes upstairs
> To sleep in strangers' blankets.
> But I opine
> The Florentine
> Who thus in strains heroic
> Bewailed his lot,
> Had quite forgot
> His sorrows at Glen Quoich.

I have since discovered a third, by Oscar Wilde:

> How steep the stairs within Kings' houses are
> For exile-wearied feet as mine to tread.

Wilde actually used this couplet twice – first in 'Ravenna' and again in his sonnet 'At Verona'. I wonder why; it's not very good.

~

Previous Crackers *have included palindromes and holo-rhymes; now it's the turn of mnemonics. All the best ones should enable one to remember basically useless information – still more useless, ideally, than the first thirty-six Roman Emperors. Paddy Leigh Fermor gave me the first two lines; and some time afterwards, lying in bed with a cold, I made up the rest.*

A truant calf calls noisily;
Great obstinate! Vile veal!
Thus dominating nervousness
Through hoarding apple-peel.
Mid-August come, persistently,
Don-Juans, sex-suffused,
Coerce mature hetairas
Anti-socially misused.
Go, go my boys! Go pandering!
Descend green Arno's valley!
Give chase! Among those flowery peaks
Can't countless numbers dally?

The initial letters give the key to the Emperors:

Augustus, Tiberius, Caligula, Claudius, Nero,
Galba, Otho, Vitellius, Vespasian,
Titus, Domitian, Nerva,
Trajan, Hadrian, Antoninus Pius,
Marcus Aurelius, Commodus, Pertinax,

Didius Julianus, Septimius Severus,
Caracalla, Macrinus, Heliogabalus,
Alexander Severus, Maximin,
Gordian, Gordian, Maximus, Balbinus, Gordian, Philip,
Decius, Gallus, Aemilianus, Valerian,
Gallienus, Claudius, Aurelian, Tacitus, Florianus, Probus,
Carus, Carinus, Numerian, Diocletian.

~

*One of the inherent dangers of keeping a commonplace book
is that of overloading it with Pepys. Here he is on 5 December
1660:*

I dined at home; and after dinner went to the new Theatre
and there I saw *The Merry Wifes of Windsor* acted. The
humours of the Country gentleman and the French
Doctor very well done; but the rest but very poorly, and
Sir J. Falstaffe as bad as any.

From thence to Mr Will Montagu's chamber to have
sealed some writings tonight between Sir R. Pankhurst
and myself, about my Lord's 2000*l.*; but he not coming,
I went to my father's. And there found my mother still ill
of the stone and hath just newly voided one, which she
hath let drop into the Chimny; and could not find it to
show it me. From thence home and to bed.

It was not Shakespeare's only failure with Pepys. On 6 January 1663 he writes:

And after dinner to the Dukes house and there saw *Twelfth Night* acted well, though it be but a silly play and not relating at all to the name or day. Thence Mr Battersby (the apothecary), his wife and I and mine by coach together, and setting him down at his house, he paying his share, my wife and I home and find all well. Only, myself somewhat vexed at my wife's neglect in leaving of her scarfe, waistcoat, and night-dressings in the coach today that brought us from Westminster, though I confess she did give them to me to look after – yet it was her fault not to see that I did take them out of the coach.

~

In the year AD 1000 the Western Emperor Otto III opened up the tomb of Charlemagne at Aix-la-Chapelle. He was accompanied by two bishops, and by Count Otto of Lomello, who left the following account (recorded by a chronicler in the monastery of Novalese in Lombardy):

We entered in unto Charles. He was not lying down, as is the manner with the bodies of other dead men, but was sitting as though he were alive, on a chair. He was crowned with a golden crown and held a sceptre in his hands, the same being covered with gloves, through which the nails had grown. And above and around him was a tabernacle of brass and marble. Now when we were come into the tomb, we broke this down to make an opening in it. And when we entered in, we were assailed by a pungent smell. And so we sank upon our bended knees before him; and straightaway Otto the Emperor clad him in white raiment, and cut his nails, and made good all that was lacking about him. But no part of his body had corrupted or fallen away, except a little piece of the end of his nose, which the Emperor caused at once to be restored with gold; and he took from his mouth one tooth, and built up the tabernacle again, and departed.

~

My friend Enid McLeod, who has a cottage on the Île de Ré, has sent me an extract from her local newspaper reproducing a letter addressed to a typewriter shop by a dissatisfied customer:

Monsixur,

Il y a quxlquxs sxmainxs jx mx suis offxrt unx dx vos machinxs à écrirx. Au début j'xn fus assxz contxnt. Mais pas pour longtxmps. Xn xffxt, vous voyxz vous-mêmx

lx défaut. Chaqux fois qux jx vxux tapxr un x, c'xst un x
qux j'obtixns. Cxla mx rxnd xnragé. Car quand jx vxux
un x, c'xst un x qu'il mx faut xt non un x. Cxla rxndrait
n'importx qui furixux. Commxnt fairx pour obtxnir un
x chaqux fois qux jx désirx un x? Un x xst un x, xt non
un x. Saisissxz-vous cx qux jx vxux dirx?

Jx voudrais savoir si vous êtxs xn mxsurx dx mx
livrxr unx machinx à écrirx donnant un x chaqux fois
qux j'ai bxsoin d'un x. Parcx qux si vous mx donnxz
unx machinx donnant un x lorsqu'on tapx un x, vous
pourrxz ravoir cx damné instrumxnt. Un x xst très bixn
tant qux x, mais, oh xnfxr!

Sincèrxmxnt à vous, un dx vos clixnts rxndu xnragé.

Xugènx X . . .

1980–1989

John Alexander Smith, Waynflete Professor of Moral and Metaphysical Philosophy at Oxford, began a course of lectures in 1914 with the following words:

Gentlemen, you are now about to embark upon a course of studies which will occupy you for two years. Together, they form a noble adventure. But I would like to remind you of an important point. Some of you, when you go down from the University, will go into the Church, or to the Bar, or to the House of Commons, or to the Home Civil Service, or the Indian or Colonial Services, or into various professions. Some may go into the Army, some into industry and commerce; some may become country gentlemen. A few – I hope a very few – will become teachers or dons. Let me make this clear to you. Except for those in the last category, nothing that you will learn in the course of your studies will be of the slightest possible use to you in after life – save only this – that if you work hard and intelligently you should be able to detect *when a man is talking rot*, and that, in my view, is the main, if not the sole, purpose of education.

Isaiah Berlin tells me that Professor Smith talked a good deal of rot himself. He was, however, according to the Dictionary of National Biography, *'skilful at card tricks and other forms of legerdemain' – which must surely count in his favour.*

~

The church of St Mary Magdalen in the Norfolk village of Mulbarton contains a most curious memorial. It is to Mrs Sarah Scargill, who died in 1680, and it takes the form of a copper diptych resting on the wooden back of a Bible. This diptych is normally closed; it can however be opened by the winding of a handle, whereupon it reveals a poem by Mrs Scargill's husband. This runs:

> Dear Love, one Feather'd minute and I come
> To lye down in thy darke Retiring Roome
> And mingle Dust with thine, that wee may have,
> As when alive one Bed, so dead one Grave;
> And may my Soul teare through the vaulted Sky
> To be with thine to all Eternitie.
> O how our Bloudless Formes will that Day greet
> With Love Divine when we again shall meet
> Devest of all Contagion of the Flesh
> Full with everlasting joys and Fresh

In Heaven above (and 't may be) cast an eye
How far Elizium doth beneath us lye.

Deare, I disbody and away
More swift than Wind
Or flying Hind
I come I come away.

~

I once wrote a book about the Sahara in which I noted:

Date palms are generally held by those who cultivate them to have a considerable capacity for affection; if one of them dies, its neighbours will mourn for it, drooping and ceasing to bear fruit. A female palm, I was told, will even pine away altogether if its lover is felled.

I have recently found corroboration of this remarkable fact in Ammianus Marcellinus. Writing in the fourth century AD about the campaigns of the Emperor Julian the Apostate in Mesopotamia (Book XXIV, Chapter 3), he notes:

Palm-trees grow there over a great extent of the country, reaching as far as Mesene and the ocean, forming extensive groves. And wherever one goes one sees continually stocks and suckers of palms, from the fruit of which an abundance of honey and wine is made, and the palms themselves are said to be divided into male and female. The two sexes, moreover, can be easily distinguished.

It is also said that the female trees produce fruit when impregnated by the seeds of the male trees, and even that they feel delight in their mutual love: and that this is clearly shown by the fact that they lean towards one another, and cannot be bent back even by strong winds. And if by any unusual accident a female tree is not impregnated by the male seed, it produces nothing but imperfect fruit; and if they cannot find out with what male tree any female tree is in love, they smear the trunk of some tree with the oil which proceeds from her, and then some other tree naturally conceives a fondness for the odour; and these proofs create some belief in the story of their copulation.

~

Gibbon has some cheerful information regarding the Emperor Gordian:

His manners were less pure, but his character was equally amiable with that of his father. Twenty-two acknowledged concubines, and a library of sixty-two thousand volumes, attested the variety of his inclinations, and from the productions which he left behind him, it appears that the former as well as the latter were designed for use rather than ostentation.

Gibbon's own library was a good deal smaller than Gordian's – a mere six thousand volumes – and on his death it was bought as a single lot by William Beckford. Beckford's motive was a curious one: spite. Some years before, Gibbon had insulted him, and he had never forgiven the offence. Now, hearing that Gibbon had left instructions that the library should be made freely available to the public, he bought it for the sole purpose of keeping it locked up. It remained in Lausanne, and only once did he ever go there to see it. Soon afterwards, he gave it away to the Swiss friend who had bought it for him. It was probably at about this time that he wrote on the endpaper of his own copy of The Decline and Fall:

The time is not far distant, Mr Gibbon, when your almost ludicrous self-complacency, your numerous, and sometimes apparently wilful mistakes, your frequent distortion of historical Truth to provoke a jibe, or excite a sneer at everything most sacred and vulnerable, your ignorance of the oriental languages, your limited and far from acutely critical knowledge of the Latin and Greek, and in the midst of all the prurient and obscene gossip of your notes – your affected moral purity perking up every now and then from the corrupt mass like artificial roses shaken off in the dark by some Prostitute on a heap of manure, your heartless scepticism, your unclassical fondness for meretricious ornament, your tumid diction, your monotonous jingle of periods, will be still more exposed and scouted than they have been. Once fairly kicked off from your lofty, bedizened stilts, you will be reduced to your just level and true standard. *W.B.*

The interesting thing about this diatribe is that every one of Beckford's arrows is accurately aimed. But Gibbon was still a superb writer – a hundred times greater than his attacker could ever hope to be.

Since the publication of the 1981 Cracker, *my friend Anthony Hobson has drawn my attention to an article of his in the April 1976 number of the* Connoisseur *which rather contradicts the story told above. Having quoted Beckford's diatribe in full, he goes on:*

In spite of this, Beckford was probably telling the truth when he said that he bought the library to read. It was rich in history and travel – both subjects that particularly interested him – and as soon as the political situation allowed, in 1802, he travelled to Lausanne, shut himself up with the books for six weeks, and read himself nearly blind.

Extracts from the Index to The Violent Effigy: A Study of Dickens' Imagination *by John Carey:*

babies, bottled, 82
boiling spirit, 25–6
cannibalism, 22–4, 175
cleanliness, excessive, 36–7
coffins, walking, 80–1
combustible persons, 14, 165
dust heaps, 109–11
fire, seeing pictures in, 16
fragmented vision, 95–8
guillotining, 20–1
home-smashing, 17
junk, enchantment of, 49–50
legs, humour of, 61–2, 92–3
mirrored episodes, 125–6
personal climates, 134–5
pokers, red-hot, 26, 85
'ruffian class', the, 38–9
scissored women, 163–4
snuff, composed of dead bodies, 80
soldiers, attraction of, 40–1
virtuous violence, 28–9
wooden legs, 91–3, 103
wooden men, 88, 102–3
zoo, feeding time at, 68–9

Apart from the fact that they prostitute their daughters, the Lydian way of life is not unlike our own.

Herodotus

~

From the Journals of Benjamin Robert Haydon:

Carew told us a capital story of the Duke. The Duke was at the Marchioness of Downshire's, and the ladies plagued him for some of his stories. For some time he declared all his stories were in print. At last he said: 'Well, I'll tell you one that has not been printed.'

In the middle of the battle of Waterloo he saw a man in plain clothes riding about on a cob in the thickest fire. During a temporary lull the Duke beckoned him, and he rode over. He asked him who he was, and what business he had there. He replied he was an Englishman, accidentally at Brussels: that he had never seen a fight and wanted to see one. The Duke told him he was in instant danger of his life; he said, 'Not more than your Grace,' and they parted. But every now and then he saw the cob-man riding about in the smoke, and at last having nobody to send to a regiment, he again beckoned to this little fellow, and told him to go up to that regiment and order them to charge – giving him some mark of authority the colonel would recognise. Away he galloped, and in a few minutes the Duke saw his order obeyed.

The Duke asked him for his card, and found in the evening, when the card fell out of his sash, that he lived at Birmingham, and was a button manufacturer! When at Birmingham the Duke enquired of the firm, and found he was their traveller, and then in Ireland. When he returned, at the Duke's request he called on him in London. The Duke was happy to see him, and said he had a vacancy in the Mint of £800 a year, where accounts were wanted. The little cob-man said it would be exactly the thing, and the Duke installed him.

~

Last year I was asked to be the reader/narrator/compère of the annual series of Christmas Carol Concerts given by the Royal Liverpool Philharmonic Society. This involved a most enjoyable search for about a dozen bits of suitably seasonal but unhackneyed material – during which I came across the following. It is by the American poet Phyllis McGinley:

All the Days of Christmas

What shall my true love
Have from me

To pleasure his Christmas
Wealthily?
The partridge has flown
From our pear tree.

Flown with our summers
Are the swans and the geese.
Milkmaids and drummers
Would leave him little peace.
I've no gold ring
And no turtle dove,
So what can I bring
To my true love?

A coat for the drizzle
Chosen at the store;
A saw and a chisel
For mending the door;
A pair of red slippers
To slip on his feet;
Three striped neckties;
Something sweet.

He shall have all
I can best afford—
No pipers, piping,
No leaping lord,
But a fine fat hen

For his Christmas board;
Two pretty daughters
(Versed in the role)

To be worn like pinks
In his buttonhole;
And the tree of my heart
With its calling linnet—
My evergreen heart
And the bright bird in it.

~

Sir Robert Baden-Powell, of Boy Scout and Mafeking fame, once wrote a book – it was first published in 1889 – called Pig-sticking or Hog-hunting; a Complete Account for Sportsmen – and Others. *On the title page there is an epigraph:*

'DUM SPIRO SPEARO' – *Old Shikari*

which must have had them in fits in the mess. I like the dedication too:

DEDICATED
by permission
to
HIS ROYAL HIGHNESS

47

THE

PRINCE OF WALES

who in the Pig-sticking field proved himself

in the fuller sense of the word

A Prince among Sportsmen

On pages 204–5 of the 1924 edition there is a section entitled 'THE PIG HIMSELF AS AN ALLY' in which we read:

Among your animal allies the pig himself is perhaps your best in making the sport the sport that it is. When reading in cold blood about pig-sticking one might naturally have an underlying suspicion of the cruelty of it to the hunted animal. But after even a brief experience of the ways and nature of the pig, one becomes convinced of the fact that he alone among animals seems to enjoy being hunted . . . He always seems glad to meet you and glad to die, which I cannot recall in the case of any animal of more sensitive temperament.

~

The French, I suspect, don't mind proper names in poetry as much as we do. Perhaps, indeed, they don't mind them at all. The second line of the following poem by Gérard de Nerval, 'Fantaisie', would surely have been unthinkable in

English; in French, it hardly seems to matter. Anyway, I find the rest of the poem so haunting that I shall quote it in full:

Il est un air pour qui je donnerais
Tout Rossini, tout Mozart et tout Weber,
Un air très vieux, languissant et funèbre,
Qui pour moi seul a des charmes secrets.

Or, chaque fois que je viens à l'entendre,
De deux cents ans mon âme rajeunit:
C'est sous Louis Treize; et je crois voir s'étendre
Un coteau vert, que le couchant jaunit,

Puis un château de brique à coins de pierre,
Aux vitraux teints de rougeâtres couleurs,
Ceint de grands parcs, avec une rivière
Baignant ses pieds, qui coule entre des fleurs;

Puis une dame, à sa haute fenêtre.
Blonde aux yeux noirs, en ses habits anciens,
Que, dans une autre existence, peut-être,
J'ai dejà vue . . . – et dont je me souviens!

~

In 1974 I included in the Cracker *a quotation from a book called* Health's Improvement: Or, Rules Comprizing and Discovering the Nature, Method and Manner of Preparing all sorts of FOOD used in this Nation, *by 'that ever Famous Thomas Muffett, Doctor in Physick'. (Dr Muffett was also, in his day, the leading authority on insects – an expertise not, alas, shared by his daughter Patience who became the world's most celebrated arachnophobe.) The following further extracts are taken from the 1655 edition, 'corrected and enlarged' by Dr Christopher Bennet, Fellow of the 'College of Physitians' in London.*

Swans flesh was forbidden the Jewes, because by them the Hieroglyphical Sages did describe hypocrisie; for as Swans have the whitest feathers and the blackest flesh of all birds, so the heart of *Hypocrites* is contrary to their outward appearance.

So that not for the badness of their flesh, but for resembling of wicked men's minds they were forbidden: for being young they are not the worst of meats; nay if they be kept in a little pound and well fed with Corn, their flesh will not only alter the blackness, but also be freed of the unwholesomeness; Being thus used, they are appointed to be the first dish at the Emperour of *Muscovie* his table, and also much esteemed in East-Friezland.

Puffins, whom I may call the feathered fishes, are accounted even by the holy fatherhood of Cardinals to be no flesh but rather fish; whose Catholique censure I will not here oppugne, though I have just reason for it, because I will not encrease the Popes Coffers; which no doubt would be filled, if every Puffin eater bought a pardon, upon true and certain knowledge that a Puffin were flesh: albeit perhaps if his Holiness would say, that a shoulder of Muton were fish, they either would not or could not think it flesh.

~

When Earth's last picture is painted and the tubes
  are twisted and dried,
When the oldest colours have faded, and the
  youngest critic has died,
We shall rest, and, faith, we shall need it – lie
  down for an aeon or two,
Till the Master of all Good Workmen shall put us
  to work anew.

And those that were good shall be happy; they
  shall sit in a golden chair;
They shall splash at a ten-league canvas with
  brushes of comets' hair.
They shall find real saints to draw from –
  Magdalene, Peter and Paul;
They shall work for an age at a sitting and never
  be tired at all!

And only The Master shall praise us, and only
   The Master shall blame;
And no one shall work for money, and no one
   shall work for fame,
But each for the joy of the working, and each, in
   his separate star,
Shall draw the Thing as he sees It for the God of
   Things as They are!

Rudyard Kipling, 'When Earth's Last Picture is Painted'

A few years ago I used this poem in a son et lumière *script I wrote for Chartwell, because it perfectly reflected Churchill's own attitude to painting. Indeed, in* Painting as a Pastime *– one of the very best things he ever wrote – he almost quoted it:*

When I get to heaven I mean to spend a considerable proportion of my first million years in painting, and so get to the bottom of the subject. But then I shall require a still gayer palette than I get here below. I expect orange and vermilion will be the darkest, dullest colours upon it and beyond them there will be a whole range of wonderful new colours which will delight the celestial eye . . .

Elsewhere in the same book he writes:

I must say I like bright colours . . . I rejoice with the brilliant ones, and am genuinely sorry for the poor browns.

~

From the second volume of Noel Coward's autobiography, Future Indefinite, *comes this description of his brief encounter with Sibelius:*

During my stay in Helsinki someone suggested that I should pay a call on Sibelius, who, although he lived a life of the utmost quiet and seclusion, would, I was assured, be more than delighted to receive me. This, later, proved to be an overstatement. However, encouraged by the mental picture of the great Master being practically unable to contain himself at the thought of meeting face to face the man who had composed 'A Room with a View' and 'Mad Dogs and Englishmen', I drove out graciously to call upon him. His house was a few miles away in the country and my guide-interpreter and I arrived there about noon. We were received by a startled, bald-headed gentleman whom I took to be an aged family retainer. He led us, without any marked signs of enthusiasm, on to a small, trellis-enclosed veranda, and left us alone. We conversed in low, reverent voices and offered each other cigarettes and waited with rising nervous tension for the Master to appear. I remember regretting bitterly my casual approach to classical music and trying frantically in my mind to disentangle the works of Sibelius from those of Delius. After about a quarter of an hour the bald-headed man reappeared carrying a tray upon which was a decanter of wine and a plate of biscuits. He put this on the table and then, to my surprise, sat down and looked at us. The silence became almost unbearable, and my friend muttered something in Finnish to which the bald-headed gentleman replied with an exasperated nod. It then dawned upon me that this was the great man himself, and furthermore that he hadn't the faintest idea who I was, who my escort was, or what we were doing there at all. Feeling embarrassed and extremely silly I smiled vacuously and offered him a cigarette, which he refused. My friend then rose, I thought a trifle officiously, and poured out three glasses of wine. We then proceeded to toast each other politely but in the same oppressive silence. I asked my friend if Mr Sibelius could speak English or French and he said 'No'. I then asked him to explain to him how very much I admired his music and what an honour it was for me to meet him personally. This was translated, upon which Sibelius rose abruptly to his feet and offered me a biscuit. I accepted it with rather overdone gratitude, and then down came the silence again, and I looked forlornly past Sibelius's head through a gap in the trellis at the road. Finally, realising that unless I did something decisive we should probably stay there until sundown, I got up and asked my friend – whom I could willingly have garrotted – to thank Mr Sibelius for receiving me and to explain once again how honoured I was to meet him, and that I hoped he would forgive us for leaving so soon but we had an appointment at the hotel for lunch. Upon this being communicated to him, Sibelius smiled for the first time and we shook hands with enthusiasm. He escorted us to the gate and waved happily as we drove away.

∼

Early in 1975, when I was editing a one-volume History of World Architecture, *I decided to commission a 600-word introduction from the renowned engineer, architect and visionary Buckminster Fuller. There arrived, almost by return of post, a 3,500-word article which built up to the following climactic conclusion:*

We will see the (1) down-at-the-mouth-ends curvature of land civilisation's retrogression from the (2) straight raft line foundation of the Mayans' building foundation lines historically transformed to the (3) smiling, up-end curvature of maritime technology transformed through the climbing angle of wingfoil aeronautics precessing humanity into the verticality of outward-bound rocketry and inward-bound microcosmy, ergo (4) the ultimately invisible and vertically-lined architecture as humans master local environment with invisible electromagnetic fields while travelling by radio as immortal pattern-integrities.

On reflection, I asked Dr Nikolaus Pevsner instead.

~

For all compilers of commonplace books, epitaphs are the most perilous of pitfalls. In a way they are too easy: if given half a chance, they tend to overload the whole collection. But they provide too rich a vein of poetry, humour and fantasy to be omitted altogether, especially ones like this:

Here lies the body of Lady O'Looney, great-niece of Burke, commonly called the sublime. She was bland, passionate, and deeply religious; also, she painted in water-colours and sent several pictures to the exhibition. She was first cousin to Lady Jones; and of such is the Kingdom of Heaven.

But the more laconic in style also have their charm. Like that in the curious little Georgian Gothic church of Tetbury in Gloucestershire which reads:

In a vault underneath
lie several of the Saunderses,
late of this parish: particulars
the Last Day will disclose.

~

When I reproduced the diabolically difficult 'Dictée de Mérimée' in 1974, everybody pointed out that French dictations were, of course, a great deal harder than English ones. So they are; but while Philip Ziegler was researching his biography of my mother, the late Sir Alan Lascelles gave him a copy of an English dictation which, he claimed, was concocted and tried out at Belvoir Castle before the First World War. Arthur Balfour is said to have made fourteen mistakes, Raymond Asquith ten. Alternative admissible spellings are given in brackets.

The most skilful gauger was a malignant cobbler, possessing a poignant disposition, who drove a pedlar's wagon (waggon), using a goad as an instrument of coercion to tyrannise (-ze) over his pony. He was a Galilean and Sadducee, and suffered from phthisical diphtheria and a bilious intermittent erysipelas. A certain sibyl with the sobriquet (soubriquet) of a gipsy (gypsy) went into ecstasy at seeing him measure some peeled potatoes and saccharine tomatoes with dyeing and singeing ignitable (-ible) materials.

On becoming paralysed with haemorrhage, lifting her eyes to the ceiling of the cupola to conceal her unparalleled embarrassment, she made a rough curtsey (curtsy), and not harassing him with mystifying rarefying innuendoes, she gave him for a couch a bouquet of lilies, mignonette, fuchsias, chrysanthemums, dahlias, a treatise on pneumonia, a copy of the Apocrypha in hieroglyphics, a daguerreotype of Mendelssohn, a kaleidoscope, a drachm (dram) of ipecacuanha, a teaspoonful of naphtha for delible purposes, a clarinet, some liquorice, a cornelian of symmetrical proportions, a chronometer with movable (moveable) balance, a box of loose dominoes and a catechism. The gauger was a trafficking parishioner who preferred the Pentateuch. His choice was reparable, vacillating, and with occasionally recurring idiosyncrasies. He woefully uttered an apothegm (apophthegm): 'Life is chequered, but schism, apostasy, heresy and villainy must be punished.' The sibyl, apologising (-izing), answered: 'There is ratably (rateably) an eligible choice between an ellipsis and a trisyllable.'

~

. . . je voudrais qu'à cet age,
On sortit de la vie ainsi que d'un banquet,
Remerciant son hôte . . .

La Fontaine

~

Sir Thomas Beecham, after conducting the 'Dance of the Cygnets' (from Swan Lake) *for the ballet of the Camargo Society at about twice the normal speed.*

That made the buggers hop.

~

In a footnote to the last chapter of Modern Painters, *John Ruskin quotes this extract from a letter written by the father of Charles Kingsley:*

I had taken my mother and a cousin to see Turner's pictures; and, as my mother knows nothing about art, I was taking her down the gallery to look at the large Richmond Park, but as we were passing the Sea-storm, she stopped before it, and I could hardly get her to look at any other picture; and she told me a great deal more about it than I had any notion of, though I have seen

59

many sea-storms. She had been in such a scene on the coast of Holland during the war. When, some time afterwards, I thanked Turner for his permission for her to see the pictures, I told him that he would not guess which had caught my mother's fancy, and then named the picture; and then he said, 'I did not paint it to be understood, but I wished to show what such a scene was like: I got the sailors to lash me to the mast to observe it; I was lashed for four hours and I did not expect to escape, but I felt bound to record it if I did. But no one had any business to like the picture.' 'But,' said I, 'my mother once went through just such a scene, and it brought it all back to her.' 'Is your mother a painter?' 'No.' 'Then she ought to have been thinking of something else.'

~

How beautiful, I have often thought, would be the names of many of our vilest diseases, were it not for their disagreeable associations. My old friend Jenny Fraser sent me this admirable illustration of the fact by J. C. Squire:

So forth then rode Sir Erysipelas
From good Lord Goitre's castle, with the steed
Loose on the rein: and as he rode he mused
On Knights and Ladies dead: Sir Scrofula,
Sciatica of Glanders, and his friend,

Stout Sir Colitis out of Aquitaine,
And Impetigo, proudest of them all,
Who lived and died for blind Queen Cholera's sake:
Anthrax, who dwelt in the enchanted wood
With those princesses three, tall, pale and dumb,
And beautiful, whose names were music's self,
Anaemia, Influenza, Eczema.
And then once more the incredible dream came back,
How long ago upon the fabulous shores
Of far Lumbago, all of a summer's day,
He and the maid Neuralgia, they twain,
Lay in a flower-crowned mead, and garlands wove,
Of gout and yellow hydrocephaly,
Dim palsies, and pyrrhoea, and the sweet
Myopia, bluer than the summer sky:
Agues, both white and red, pied common cold,
Cirrhosis and that wan, faint flower
The shepherds call dyspepsia. – Gone, all gone:
There came a Knight: he cried 'Neuralgia!'
And never a voice to answer. Only rang
O'er cliff and battlement and desolate mere
'Neuralgia!' in the echoes' mockery.

1990—1999

One of the most curious footnotes to history I know is that which concerns the fate of the heart of Louis XIV. I quote from a letter received a few years ago from my friend Quentin Crewe:

As I think I told you, while the bodies of the Kings of France were buried at the church of St Denis, the hearts used to go to a church in the Loiret. Anne of Austria, the wife of Louis XIII, instituted a new practice. She built Val de Grâce, and it became the new repository for royal hearts. (Incidentally, I believe she crawled from the Bishop's Palace in Apt to the Cathedral there, in order to pray before the bones of St Anne for a son.) Her heart, Charles I's wife's heart and, ultimately, Louis XIV's heart were put in silver cases in Val de Grâce. It was in the scrum outside the church during the Revolution that a member of the Harcourt family found himself holding the case with Louis XIV's heart in it.

In the Harcourt papers, there is an inventory of the contents of Nuneham Manor. It says that in the drawing room there is 'a small case which formerly contained a portion of the heart of Louis XIV, obtained at Val de

Grâce when spoliation took place during the French Revolution'. The papers do not say what happened to the heart. They merely state that 'the case still remains, but the contents came to an extraordinary ending in 1848'. The family story was that Dr William Buckland, Dean of Westminster, who was also a mineralogist holding the Chair at Oxford, came to dinner. It was his boast that he could tell any mineral by its taste. The heart looked a little like a piece of pumice stone by this time; Buckland was blindfolded and given it as a joke to identify. He was so shocked by the taste of formaldehyde that he gasped, swallowed the heart by mistake, and – according to one version of the story – died the same night.

The last point is in fact inaccurate: Buckland lived on until 1856. The silver case – now of course empty – still lies on a chest in the dining room, beneath a portrait of Dr Buckland. There is also a contemporary poem entitled 'Conversation at Dinner, 1848'; the poem relates the story and ends with these lines:

Here lives a Very Reverend shade,
   A man of parts,
Who holds until the last trump's played,
   The Ace of Hearts.

~

An announcement in the Cork Examiner*:*

Donnachie's Bar, Cobh. Due to the sad death of Paddy, the Bar, to all intents and purposes, will remain closed during our grief; but so as not to inconvenience our esteemed customers, the door will remain ajar. 'Tis what Paddy wanted. Thank you. The Donnachie family.

~

Sydney Smith's recipe for a salad:

To make this condiment your poet begs
The pounded yellow of two hard-boil'd eggs;
Two boiled potatoes, passed through kitchen sieve,
Smoothness and softness to the salad give.
Let onion atoms lurk within the bowl,
And, half-suspected, animate the whole.
Of mordant mustard add a single spoon,
Distrust the condiment that bites so soon;
But deem it not, thou man of herbs, a fault
To add a double quantity of salt;
Four times the spoon with oil of Lucca crown,
And twice with vinegar, procur'd from town;
And lastly o'er the flavour'd compound toss
A magic *soupçon* of anchovy sauce.
Oh, green and glorious! Oh, herbaceous treat!

'Twould tempt the dying anchorite to eat;
Back to the world he'd turn his fleeting soul,
And plunge his fingers in the salad-bowl!
Serenely full, the epicure would say,
'Fate cannot harm me, I have dined today.'

And one by my father, more characteristically, for a cocktail:

Rum, divine daughter of the sugar cane,
Rum, staunch ally of those who sail the sea,
Jamaican rum of rarest quality!
One half of rum the goblet shall contain.
Bring Andalusian oranges from Spain,
And lemons from the groves of Sicily;
Mingle their juices (proportions two to three)
And sweeten all with Demeraran grain.
Of Angosturan bitters just a hint,
And, for the bold, of brandy just a spice,
A leaf or two of incense-bearing mint,
And any quantity of clinking ice:
Then shake, then pour, then quaff, and never stint,
Till life shall seem a dream of Paradise.

This sonnet won a New Statesman *Weekend Competition.
I still possess the glass shaker on which he lavished his
winnings, and on which the verse is inscribed.*

Reflection on life:

> The rain it raineth every day
> Upon the just and unjust fella,
> But chiefly on the just, because
> The unjust steals the just's umbrella.

Charles Bowen

~

How to compose operatic overtures: a letter from Gioachino Rossini, giving advice to a young colleague:

Wait till the evening before the opening night. Nothing primes inspiration like necessity, whether it takes the form of a copyist waiting for your work or the coercion of an exasperated impresario tearing his hair out in handfuls. In my day all the impresarios in Italy were bald at thirty.

I wrote the overture to *Otello* in a little room at the Barbaja Palace, in which the baldest and fiercest of these impresarios had locked me by force with nothing but a plate of *maccheroni* and the threat that I should not leave the room alive until I had written the last note. I wrote the overture to *La Gazza Ladra* on the day of the first performance in the theatre itself, where I was imprisoned by the director and watched over by four

stage-hands, who had instructions to throw my manuscript out of the window page by page to the copyists
who were waiting to transcribe it below. In the absence
of pages, they were to throw me.

With the *Barber* I did better still. I didn't compose an
overture, but simply took one which had been meant for an
opera semiseria called *Elisabetta*. The public was delighted.

The overture to *Conte Ory* I wrote while fishing, with
my feet in the water, in the company of Signor Aguado
who was talking about Spanish finance. The one for
William Tell was done under more or less similar circumstances. As for *Mosè*, I just didn't write one at all.

~

I stopped believing in Santa Claus when I was six.
Mother took me to see him in a department store and he
asked for my autograph.

Shirley Temple

~

Alternative Endings to an Unwritten Ballad

I stole through the dungeons, while everyone slept,
Till I came to the cage where the Monster was kept.

There, locked in the arms of a Giant Baboon,
Rigid and smiling, lay . . . MRS RAVOON!

I climbed the clock-tower in the first morning sun
And 'twas midday at least ere my journey was done;
But the clock never sounded the last stroke of noon,
For there, from the clapper, swung MRS RAVOON.

I hauled in the line, and I took my first look
At the half-eaten horror that hung from the hook.
I had dragged from the depths of the limpid lagoon
The luminous body of MRS RAVOON.

I fled in the storm, through the lightning and thunder,
And there, as a flash split the darkness asunder,
Chewing a rat's-tail and mumbling a rune,
Mad in the moat squatted MRS RAVOON.

I stood by the waters so green and so thick,
And I stirred at the scum with my old, withered stick;
When there rose through the ooze, like a monstrous
    balloon,
The bloated cadaver of MRS RAVOON.

Facing the fens, I looked back from the shore
Where all had been empty a moment before;
And there, by the light of the Lincolnshire moon,
Immense on the marshes stood . . . MRS RAVOON!

*Mrs Ravoon was first introduced to me by Linda Kelly,
though she was actually the creation of the late Paul Dehn;
she made her début in his book* The Fern on the Rock. *After
that she was unstoppable: what Dehn described as 'Ravoon
sightings' continued. Sometimes they were his own as in:*

As a whaler, I knew I was meeting my match,
But I heaved on the rope and I landed my catch.
Transfixed by the spike of the bloody harpoon,
Nodding and smiling, twitched MRS RAVOON.

*and sometimes those of others, long after his death in 1976.
Two recent examples:*

A torch flickered, deep in the Valley of Kings:
'I see', whispered Carter, 'oh, wonderful things!'
'Do you think,' gasped Carnarvon, 'it's Tutankhamun?'
Then it sat up and leered: it was . . . MRS RAVOON.

and

Below the salt Channel they're drinking champagne
And ministers jostle to board the first train.
Emergency bells ring in French and Walloon,
For there on the buffers squats . . . MRS RAVOON.

~

*An Elizabethan conceit, said to be by Sir Walter Ralegh,
and typical of the sixteenth-century love of ingenious word-
play. It can be read either vertically or horizontally – and
probably in several other ways as well:*

Her face	Her tongue	Her wit
So faire	So sweete	So sharpe
First bent	Then drew	Then hit
Mine eye	Mine eare	My heart
Mine eye	Mine eare	My heart
To like	To learne	To love
Her face	Her tongue	Her wit
Doth lead	Doth teach	Doth move
Oh face	Oh tongue	Oh wit
With frownes	With cheeke	With smarte
Wrong not	Vex not	Wound not
Mine eye	Mine eare	My heart
Mine eye	Mine eare	My heart
To learne	To knowe	To feare
Her face	Her tongue	Her wit
Doth lead	Doth teach	Doth sweare

~

I have not received many abusive letters in my life – a fact which makes this one all the more precious to me. It was written in consequence of a radio programme in which, many years ago, I acted as narrator. The writer signed it with his full name, and gave his address.

Sir,

Your brief sketch of Lord Edward Fitzgerald on Sunday night, apart from being an almost total distortion of the truth, was grossly offensive.

I realise that your employment as token peer in residence at the BBC merely required you to promulgate the prejudiced ignorance of [the author], who, as a true child of this venial age, can find no other explanation for true altruism than stupidity. Nevertheless in associating yourself with her egregious and ill-researched opinions you have not only impugned your own honour but have also gratuitously damaged the memory of one of the brightest ornaments of that caste to which I presume the Coopers [my own family] still hopefully aspire.

In the more spacious days in which Lord Edward lived you would have been made to answer for your insults on the field of honour, although in my view you demeaned yourself to a degree that would make a horse-whipping more appropriate.

I suggest the BBC mount a full-length programme on the life of Lord Edward in recompense for last

Sunday's slander. If it did nothing else, such a programme would bring some of you face to face with the realities of physical and moral courage as well as true integrity and selflessness; a revelatory adventure into the unknown for most of you, I have no doubt.

Yours faithfully . . .

Lord Edward (1763–98) was an early champion of Irish independence. He died in Newgate prison, of wounds received when resisting arrest. 'Moore, who once saw him in 1797, speaks of his peculiar dress, elastic gait, healthy complexion, and the soft expression given to his eyes by long, dark eyelashes.' (DNB)

~

It was Hester up in Chester, it was Jenny down in Kent;
Up and down the motorways, the same where'er he
    went.
In Luton it was Sally, quite the nicest of the bunch,
But down on his expenses they were petrol, oil and
    lunch.

Anon.

Here are a few items extracted from the catalogue of the sale (twenty-sixth day) of the Bullock Museum in 1819, at which were sold a number of objects formerly the property of Napoleon and taken after Waterloo.

The Emperor's Personal Wardrobe, Taken in the Carriage

80: His ordinary travelling Cap of Green Velvet. [£5.6.0, Chamberlain]

82: A pair of White Silk Stockings, with the Imperial Crest on the clock (a crown). [£2.2.0, Chamberlain]

90: A very fine Cambric Pocket-handkerchief, handsomely embroidered with the N in the corner [£2.2.0, Capt. Campbell-Brooke]

95: A pair of Braces. [£0.16.0, Clift]

96: A Diaper Towel, marked N-10. [£1.2.0, Do.]

98: Another marked L. and crown, which probably belonged to Louis XVIII. [£1.0.0, Riddell]

99: Flesh-brush. [£0.15.0, Trevallion]

100: Green silk Pincushion, filled with sweet-scented wood. [£1.1.0, Bailey]

105: Set of Chessmen in a round wooden box, used by the Emperor in the Russian campaign. [£2.9.0, Lincoln]

The two massive Silver Articles of personal convenience, used in the carriage, will be disposed of by Private Contract.

[£31.10.0, The Prince Regent]

HRH The Prince of Wales has himself confirmed that they are at Windsor, where they are kept in a cupboard in the Grand Vestibule, on the way to the Waterloo Chamber.

~

It was my son-in-law Antony Beevor who showed me this splendid passage in Reflections in a Silver Spoon *by Paul Mellon:*

There was a forbidding quality in Father's cold attitude that always unnerved me and made it very difficult for me to pursue a personal conversation with him.

I sincerely believe, however, that the problem of communication rested with him as much as with me. To cite an example, he had written me a Christmas letter in 1929 from his Massachusetts Avenue apartment. It read:

Dear Paul,

As a birthday gift to you on reaching your majority last year I transferred to you 1000 shares preferred stock of the Aluminum Co. of America, as an outright gift.

Lately I transferred to you 2000 shares of the Monongahela St. Railway Co. This Monongahela St. Ry. stock is a gift to you which I make in consideration of your having given up or relinquished to your mother your interest or share in the Trust fund designated as Trust No. 3 of which the Union Trust Co. of Pittsburgh, Mr McCrory and I were Trustees. As you gave this to your mother at my instance I have made it up to you by gift of this stock.

With much love – Father

I think Father was trying in his own way in this letter to express his affection for me.

~

In 1854 the Government of the United States sought to buy a vast tract of land from one of the western Indian tribes. The chief, whose name was Sealth, or Seattle, replied in a long oration known as Chief Seattle's Testimony. Here is an extract, kindly sent me by David Attenborough:

We are a part of the earth and it is part of us. The perfumed flowers are our sisters;

The deer, the horse, the great eagle,
These are our brothers.
The rocky crests, the juices of the meadows,
The body heat of the pony, and man
– All belong to the same family.

So, when the Great Chief in Washington sends word
That he wishes to buy our land, he asks much of us . . .

We will consider your offer to buy our land.
If we decide to accept, I will make one condition:
The white man must treat the beasts of this land
As his brothers.

I am a savage and I do not understand any other way.
I have seen a thousand rotting buffalos on the prairie,
Left by the white man who shot them from a passing train.
I am a savage and I do not understand how the smoking
Iron horse can be more important than the buffalo
That we kill only to stay alive.

What is the man without the beasts?
If the beasts were gone, man would die from a great
Loneliness of spirit. For whatever happens to the beasts
Soon happens to man. All things are connected.

This we know. The earth does not belong to man;
Man belongs to the earth.

This we know. All things are connected like the blood
Which unites one family.
All things are connected.

Whatever befalls the earth befalls the sons of the earth.
Man did not weave the web of life, he is merely a strand
   in it.
Whatever he does to the web, he does to himself.

~

A letter to The Times, *published on 6 March 1985:*

Sir,

Miss Catherine J. Clark (March 2) need agonise no
longer over the etiquette governing revolving doors.
Whenever faced by this problem and a lady is about to
approach the doors, I boldly enter first and push the
doors for her; but in order to give the lady precedence
of ingress I describe a full circle before effecting my
final entry. This seems to puzzle hotel porters, but it is a
clear statement, Sir, that chivalry is not dead.

Yours faithfully
Carlo Ardito

Seventy is wormwood,
Seventy is gall,
But it's better to be 70
Than not alive at all.

*So wrote Phyllis McGinley on her seventieth birthday, but
Thornton Wilder, on his, was a good deal more up-beat:*

I was an old man when I was twelve; and now I *am* an
old man, *and it's splendid.*

~

How the Helpmate of Blue-Beard
Made Free with a Door

A maiden from the Bosphorus with eyes as bright as
  phosphorus
Once wed the wealthy bailiff of the Caliph of Kelat;
Though diligent and zealous, he became a slave to jealousy.
(Considering her beauty, 'twas his duty to be that!)

When business would necessitate a journey, he would
  hesitate,
But, fearing to disgust her, he would trust her with his
  keys,

Remarking to her prayerfully, 'I beg you'll use them
    carefully;
Don't look what I deposit in that closet, if you
    please!'

It may be mentioned, casually, that blue as lapis lazuli
He dyed his hair, his lashes, his moustaches and his
    beard;
And just because he did it, he aroused his wife's
    timidity –
Her terror she dissembled, but she trembled when he
    neared.

This feeling insalubrious soon made her most
    lugubrious,
And bitterly she missed her elder sister, Marie Anne:
She asked if she might write her to come down and
    spend a night or two?
Her husband answered rightly – and politely – 'Yes,
    you can!'

Blue-Beard, the Monday following, his jealous feelings
    swallowing,
Packed all his clothes together in a leather-bound
    valise,
And feigning reprehensibly, he started off, ostensibly
By travelling, to learn a bit of Smyrna and of Greece.

His wife made but a cursory inspection of the nursery;
The kitchen and the airy little dairy were a bore;
As well as big or scanty rooms, and billiard, bath and
    ante-rooms;
But not that interdicted and restricted little door!

For, all her curiosity awakened by the closet he
So carefully had hidden and forbidden her to see,
This damsel disobedient did something inexpedient –
And in the keyhole tiny turned the shiny little key:

Then, standing back impulsively, and shrieked aloud
    convulsively –
Three heads, of girls he'd wedded and beheaded, met
    her eye!
And turning round, much terrified, her darkest fears
    were verified;
For Blue-Beard stood behind her – come to find her on
    the sly!

Perceiving she was fated to be soon decapitated, too,
She telegraphed her brothers and some others what she
    feared;
And sister Anne looked out for them in readiness to
    shout for them
Whenever in the distance with assistance they
    appeared.

But only from her battlement she saw some dust that
    cattle meant . . .
The ordinary story isn't gory, but a jest;
But here's the truth unqualified: the husband *wasn't*
    mollified –
Her head is in his bloody little study, with the rest!

Guy Wetmore Carryl

~

Snubs:

*The fifth Earl of Dysart, to George III angling for an invi-
tation to visit his house at Ham:*

'Whenever my house becomes a public spectacle, His
Majesty shall certainly have the first view.'

Talleyrand, to a young man boasting of his mother's beauty:

'C'était donc monsieur votre père qui n'était pas beau.'

Politesse:

Vincenzo Valdrati, or Valdré (1742–1814), was an Italian
painter-architect who came to England in the 1770s and

designed, *inter alia*, several of the state rooms at Stowe before settling in Ireland, where he became Architect to the Board of Works. From Howard Colvin's superb *Biographical Dictionary of British Architects* I learn that 'while at Stowe he attended a wedding in the neighbourhood and, when the bridegroom failed to appear, chivalrously offered himself as a substitute – and was accepted'.

~

My friend Tony Sutcliffe sends me an epitaph from Lydford, Devon:

Here lies, in horizontal position,
the outside case of
GEORGE ROUTLEIGH, Watchmaker,
Whose abilities in that line were an honour
to his profession.
Integrity was the Mainspring, and prudence the
Regulator
Of all the actions of his life.
Humane, generous and liberal
his Hand never stopped
till he had relieved distress.
So nicely regulated were all his motions,
that he never went wrong,
except when set a-going

by people
who did not know his Key;
Even then he was easily
set right again.
He had the art of disposing his time so well,
that his hours glided away
in one continual round
of pleasure and delight,
until an unlucky minute put a period
to his existence.
He departed this life,
Nov. 14, 1802,
aged 57:
wound up,
in hopes of being taken in hand
by his Maker;
and of being thoroughly cleaned, repaired,
and set a-going
in the world to come.

~

The greatest pleasure I know is to do a good action by
stealth and have it found out by accident.

Charles Lamb

2000—2009

My paternal grandfather was, I learn from the OED, *a nimgimmer – a Doctor, Surgeon or Apothecary, or anyone that cures a Clap or the Pox. Here, slightly abridged but in no way censored, is his entry in the old* DNB:

COOPER, Sir Alfred (1838–1908), surgeon, born at Norwich on 28 Dec. 1838, was son of William Cooper, at one time recorder of Ipswich, by his wife Anne Marsh . . . In 1858 Cooper entered as a student at St Bartholomew's Hospital. He was admitted MRCS England on 29 June 1861.*

He then went to Paris in company with (Sir) Thomas Smith to improve his anatomical knowledge, and on his return was appointed a prosector to the examiners at the Royal College of Surgeons.

Cooper started practice in Jermyn Street. After an interval of waiting he acquired a fashionable private practice. But his social success rather stimulated than retarded his ardour for surgery. He was surgeon to St Mark's Hospital for Fistula, City Road, from April 1864 to 1897 . . . and to the Lock Hospital, Soho. At the last institution he gained that sound knowledge of syphilis with which his name is chiefly associated . . .

Cooper, whose social qualities were linked with fine traits of character and breadth of view, gained a wide knowledge of the world, partly at courts, partly in the out-patient rooms of hospitals, and partly in the exercise of a branch of his profession which more than any other reveals the frailty of mankind . . .

Cooper's works are: 1. *Syphilis and Pseudo-Syphilis*, 1884; 2nd edn. 1895.[†] 2. *A Practical Treatise on Disease of the Rectum*, 1887; 2nd edn., with Mr F. Swinford Edwards, entitled *Diseases of the Rectum and Anus*, 1892.

---

[*] Three years' training seems to have been thought enough in those days.

[†] I am the proud possessor of a copy of this, profusely illustrated in colour, but I show it only to those of sturdy constitution – and never after dinner.

Perhaps not altogether surprisingly, he numbered King Edward VII among his patients. He married above himself: Lady Agnes Duff was the daughter of the fifth Earl of Fife. Alas, by the time she met Dr Cooper at the age of twenty-eight she had notched up two elopements and a divorce. It was said that together they knew more about the private parts of the British aristocracy than any other couple in the country. I am proud to be their grandson.

Some years ago the late and sorely missed Maggie Jencks (née Keswick) sent me a copy of the earliest – but for all I know still official – translation of the Japanese Highway Code, *as delivered to her grandmother in Yokohama when she became the first woman in Japan to hold a driving licence.*

Rules of the Road in Japan

- At the rise of the hand of a policeman, stop rapidly. Do not pass him by or otherwise disrespect him.
- When a passenger of the foot hove in sight, tootle the horn trumpet to him melodiously at first. If he still obstacles your passage, tootle him with vigour and express by word of mouth the warning, 'Hi, Hi'.
- Beware of the wandering horse that shall not pass and take fright as you pass him. Do not explode the (explode) exhaust box at him. Go soothingly by, or stop by the road-way till he pass away.
- Give big space to the festive dog that makes sport in the roadway. Avoid entanglement of the dog with your wheelspokes.
- Go soothingly on the grease-mud, as there lurk the skid demon. Press the brake of the foot as you roll around the corners to save the collapse and tie-up.

~

To Anthea, Who May
Command Him Any Thing

Bid me to live, and I will live
    Thy protestant to be;
Or bid me love, and I will give
    A loving heart to thee.

A heart as soft, a heart as kind,
    A heart as sound and free
As in the whole world thou canst find,
    That heart I'll give to thee.

Bid that heart stay, and it will stay,
    To honour thy decree;
Or bid it languish quite away,
    And 't shall do so for thee.

Bid me to weep, and I will weep,
    While I have eyes to see;
And having none, yet I will keep
    A heart to weep for thee.

Bid me despair, and I'll despair,
    Under that cypress tree:
Or bid me die, and I will dare
    E'en Death, to die for thee.

Thou art my life, my love, my heart,
    The very eyes of me,
And hast command of every part,
    To live and die for thee.

There, it seems to me, is Robert Herrick at his best; but at his worst – oh dear . . .

Fain would I kiss my Julia's dainty leg
Which is as white and hairless as an egg.

~

From The Week, *8 January 2000.*

The land-locked country Swaziland has lost its entire merchant navy. The fleet, which consists of just one ship, has disappeared. But Transport Minister Ephraem Magagula is not worried. 'The situation is absolutely under control. We believe it is in the sea somewhere,' he told the *Johannesburg Star* in 2000. 'At one time we sent a team of men to look for it, but there was a problem with drink and they failed to find it. But I categorically reject all suggestions of incompetence on the part of this government. The *Swazimar* is a big ship painted in the sort of nice bright colours you can see at night. Mark my words, it will turn up.'

From the autobiography of the cellist, Paul Tortelier:

Pau [his pianist daughter] and I gave a recital at Marlborough College in Wiltshire on a particularly pleasant autumn evening. Already during the Brahms E minor Sonata, which opened the programme, I noticed a slight shadow that flickered from time to time across the brightly lit floor. And when I began playing my own Cello Sonata I was aware of something coming towards me from above, and then floating away again. It was there, and yet not there, like an apparition. While playing, I had little time to give my attention to it, but by the time I reached the middle movement of my sonata I was able to identify my mysterious stage companion. It was a butterfly – a beautifully coloured, rather big butterfly. It began to circle around me and, as it did so, it seemed almost to be tracing arabesques to the music I was playing, its wings moving in harmony with my bow.

The audience's attention had now been drawn to this wholly unrehearsed ballet. Closer and closer the butterfly would come, almost touch me, and then fly away. It was having a flirtation with me, or perhaps I with it. The slow movement of my sonata concludes quietly on a sustained harmonic. At that moment I closed my eyes, my bow barely moving on the string. I did not want to disturb the atmosphere of peace and calm. As I slowly drew the note to an end I opened my eyes and there, perched on my left hand, was the butterfly. It had alighted so gently that I hadn't felt its presence. For a moment or two we looked at each other. It didn't move; I didn't move. It was so lovely, so ethereal, that I couldn't bring myself to shake it off. It had chosen the ideal moment for repose, I thought, settling there at the end of the slow movement; it seemed not to want to fly away. What could I do? Almost without thinking, I slowly brought my hand, with the butterfly still perched on it, up to my lips. I was sure it would fly away, but it didn't. I kissed it very tenderly, but still it didn't move. Not everyone has been able to kiss a butterfly. I never thought I would do so, least of all on the concert stage. Finally I shook my hand very gently, and it floated off into the air. That was just before the interval. After the interval we played Beethoven's A major Sonata, and there was the butterfly again, dancing all the way through, only coming down to rest from time to time on Pau's music, as if wanting to have a look at what she was doing. The piece came to an end and the butterfly was nowhere to be seen. 'Aha', I thought, 'it has left us to join the other butterflies in the fields.' Not at all. It was perched on my foot, and as the audience applauded it flapped its wings.

Who can judge what forces of spirit or nature guide our actions and bring harmony to seemingly disparate things? Such forces are there, that's all I need to know. The audience that day knew it also. We had all lived a fairy tale.

A letter from Dickens to his clockmaker:

My dear Sir,

Since my hall clock was sent to your establishment to be cleaned it has gone (as indeed it always has) perfectly well, but has struck the hours with great reluctance, and after enduring internal agonies of a most distressing nature, it has now ceased striking altogether. Though a happy release for the clock, this is not convenient to the household. If you can send down any confidential person with whom the clock can confer, I think it may have something on its works it would be glad to make a clean breast of.

Faithfully yours
Charles Dickens

~

Question 3A of the application form for New York University reads: 'In order for the admissions staff of our College to get to know you, the applicant, better, we ask that you answer the following question: Are there any significant experiences you have had, or accomplishments you have realised, that have helped to define you as a person?' An applicant replied:

I am a dynamic figure, often seen scaling walls and crushing ice. I have been known to remodel train stations in my lunch breaks, making them more efficient in the area of heat return. I translate ethnic slurs for Cuban refugees, I write award-winning operas, I manage time efficiently.

Occasionally, I tread water for three days in a row.

I woo women with my sensuous and godlike trombone playing, I can pilot bicycles up severe inclines with unflagging speed, and I cook thirty-minute brownies in twelve minutes. I am an expert in stucco, a veteran in love, and an outlaw in Peru.

Using only a hoe and a large glass of water, I once single-handedly defended a small village in the Amazon basin from a horde of ferocious army ants. I play bluegrass cello, I was scouted by the Mets, I am the subject of numerous documentaries. When I'm bored, I build large suspension bridges in my yard. I enjoy urban hang gliding. On Wednesdays, after school, I repair electrical appliances free of charge.

I am an abstract artist, a concrete analyst, and a ruthless bookie. Critics world-wide swoon over my original line of corduroy evening wear. I don't perspire. I am a private citizen, yet I receive fan mail. I have been caller number nine and have won the weekend passes. Last summer I toured New Jersey with a travelling centrifugal-force demonstration. I bat 400.

My deft floral arrangements have earned me fame in international botany circles. Children trust me.

I can hurl tennis rackets at small moving objects with deadly accuracy. I once read *Paradise Lost*, *Moby Dick* and *David Copperfield* in one day and still had time to refurbish an entire dining room that evening. I know the exact location of every food item in the supermarket. I have performed several covert operations with the CIA. I sleep once a week; when I do sleep, I sleep in a chair. While on vacation in Canada, I successfully negotiated with a group of terrorists who had seized a small bakery. The laws of physics do not apply to me.

I balance, I weave, I dodge, I frolic, and my bills are all paid. On weekends, to let off steam, I participate in full-contact origami. Years ago I discovered the meaning of life but forgot to write it down. I have made extraordinary four-course meals using only a mouli and a toaster oven.

I breed prize-winning clams. I have won bullfights in San Juan, cliff-diving competitions in Sri Lanka, and spelling bees at the Kremlin.

I have played Hamlet, have performed open-heart surgery, and have spoken with Elvis.

But I have not yet gone to college.

He got in.

~

Anya Sainsbury has introduced me to Our Ballet, *by Alexander Pleshcheev, which contains this remarkable story:*

Marie Taglioni left Russia for the last time in March 1842, and the contents of her house were sold by auction. Among the goods was a pair of ballet shoes, which realised 200 roubles. These shoes were cooked, served with a special sauce and eaten at a dinner organised by a group of balletomanes.

~

Licensed Victuallers'
Home for the Aged
Bevendean Road
Brighton, Sussex

19 December 1974

Dear John,

I want to thank you for your lovely gift of a table radio. It is wonderful that an absolute stranger as yourself to remember people like us.

I am 82 years of age, and has been in the home for 16 years. They treat us very well but the loneliness is sometimes very hard to bear. My room mate Mrs

Ernstadt who is a very nice person, but she is very self-ish. She has a table radio, but she will not let me use it, she turns it off when I come into the room, now I have one of my own.

My son and daughter in law are very nice and they come & visit me once a month. I appreciate it, but I know they come out of a sense of duty & obligation. This is why your gift is all the more welcome, because it was given, not from a sense of duty, but more a feeling of compassion for a fellow human-being.

Today Mrs Ernstadt's radio went out of order & she asked me whether she could listen to mine. I told her to go and fuck herself.

Yours sincerely,
Mrs Greenfield

~

Book beginnings: among the worst, I should certainly include the opening sentence of The Last Days of Pompeii, *by Edward Bulwer-Lytton:*

'Ho, Diomed, well met! Do you sup with Glaucus tonight?' said a young man of small stature, who wore his tunic in those loose and effeminate folds which proved him to be a gentleman and a coxcomb.

Among the best, how about that of Earthly Powers, *by Anthony Burgess?*

It was the afternoon of my eighty-first birthday, and I was in bed with my catamite when Ali announced that the archbishop had come to see me.

~

As you grow old, you lose interest in sex, your friends drift away, your children often ignore you. There are many other advantages of course, but these would seem to me to be the outstanding ones.

Richard Needham, The Times, 11 November 2002

~

Sir John Gilbert, son of Sir Humphrey Gilbert the founder of Newfoundland, accompanied his uncle Sir Walter Ralegh to Guiana in 1595 and brought back a parrot, which he sent to Queen Elizabeth at her request. It was accompanied by the following letter, which was addressed to Sir Robert Cecil, Principal Secretary of State, and was dated 27 April 1596:

I have sent this bearer, my servant, of purpose unto you with the parakito, and have given him a great charge for the carrying of him. He will eat all kinds of meat and nothing will hurt him except it be very salt. If you put him on the table at meal time he will make choice of his meat. He must be kept very warm, and after he hath filled himself he will set in a gentlewoman's ruff all the day. In the afternoon he will eat bread or oatmeal groats, drink water or claret wine; every night he is put in the cage and covered warm. My servant more at large will tell you of all his conditions and qualities. Surely if he be well taught he will speak anything.

I can't quite resist comparing this letter with another, written – with, in its way, a similar purpose – to Pope Julius II:

The bearer of these gifts is Michelangelo the sculptor. His nature is such that he has to be drawn out by kindness and encouragements, but if he is treated well and if love be shown to him, he will accomplish things that will make the whole world wonder.

~

Here is a piece kindly sent me by Isabella Gardiner on the subject of Hell. It seems that a chemistry mid-term examination paper set by the University of Washington contained a bonus question: 'Is Hell exothermic (gives off heat) or endothermic (absorbs heat)?' A student submitted the following answer:

First, we need to know how the mass of Hell is changing in time. So we need to know the rate at which souls are moving into Hell and the rate at which they are leaving.

I think that we can safely assume that once a soul gets to Hell it will not leave. Therefore, no souls are leaving.

As for how many souls are entering Hell, let's look at the different religions that exist in the world today. Some of these religions state that if you are not a member of their religion you will go to Hell. Since there are more than one of these religions and since people do not belong to more than one religion, we can project that all souls go to Hell. With birth and death rates as they are, we can expect the number of souls in Hell to increase exponentially.

Now we look at the rate of change in the volume of Hell, because Boyle's law states that in order for the temperature and pressure to stay the same, the volume has to expand proportionately as souls are added.

This gives two possibilities:

1. If Hell is expanding at a slower rate than the rate at which souls enter Hell, then the temperature and pressure in Hell will increase until all Hell breaks loose.

2. If Hell is expanding at a rate faster than the increase of souls in Hell, then the temperature and pressure will drop until Hell freezes over.

So which is it?

If we accept the postulate given me by Teresa during my freshman year, that 'it will be a cold day in Hell before I sleep with you', and take into account the fact that I still have not succeeded in having sexual relations with her, then No. 2 cannot be true; and thus I am sure that Hell is endothermic and will not freeze.

The author received, we are told, the only 'A' given.

Michael Pakenham has submitted an alternative, which I prefer:

'If we accept the postulate given me by Teresa during my freshman year, that "it will be a cold day in Hell before I sleep with you",' and take account of the fact that I slept with her last night, then the second possibility must be true. This proves that Hell is exothermic and has already frozen over.

The corollary of this theory is that since Hell has frozen over, it follows that it is no longer accepting any more souls and is therefore extinct. This leaves only Heaven, thereby proving the existence of a Divine being.

Which in turn explains why last night Teresa kept shouting 'Oh my God!'

~

A few years ago there was a fashion for one-line jokes embroidered on cushions; but I was quite surprised, when visiting recently the house of Dr and Mrs Tan in Singapore, to see upon their sofa a cushion on which was inscribed:

Tolerability makes all the
difference in inflammatory acne.

~

From the address by Sir James Beament at the memorial service, held on 13 October 1992, of the Cambridge physicist Shirley Falloon:

After the war he returned to Cambridge and worked in the Radio Group under John Ratcliffe in the Cavendish Laboratory. It is difficult to imagine two more disparate characters than Falloon and Ratcliffe; indeed I am told that Ratcliffe often referred to him, in the insurance company's parlance, as an Act of God ... Ratcliffe thought to defeat Falloon's ingenuity by asking him to devise something for the 1954 Physical Society conference which would prevent even the most distinguished speakers from over-running their time. The sight of the device Shirley placed on the bench and known as the Auto Cor Strike a Light so terrified speakers that it was left to Ratcliffe's closing speech to demonstrate its awesome properties. When the Chairman pressed a button a loud spark lit a Bunsen burner. This heated a boiler which first blew a whistle and then powered a steam engine which drew back a large hammer. That in turn struck a huge tuning fork whose vibration excited a device which switched on a low voltage transformer. And that ignited a thunderflash. As several people have observed, the great difference between Shirley Falloon and Heath Robinson was that Shirley's improbable devices and ideas not only worked, but in the best sense of the practical joke were always carefully calculated so as never to be a danger to anyone. For example, when the late Ken Machin was asked by the Philharmonic Society to provide maroons in King's Chapel for the Berlioz Funeral Pieces, it was Shirley who checked the sums to ensure the safety of the famous windows – and who also saw to it that when they were discharged they left behind a fine smell of sulphur . . .

Later, he was Chairman of the University Gliding Club for six years, during which he guided the critical negotiations that transferred its activities from Marshall's Airport to Duxford. Older members of that club will however remember him above all for a particular

November 5th when various gliding clubs were invited by the Luton club to their annual party on Dunstable Downs. Each club was asked to bring a firework. The Falloon Molecular Land Mine, as it became known, did indeed start with a simple penny firework, from whose blue touch paper the igniter retired in great haste because it burned through the critical piece of string which suspended a large bucket of liquid oxygen over an open drum of petrol. The resulting explosion was seen and heard over many miles, including by the local Fire Brigade. They were not asked again.

~

The Life That I Have

The life that I have
Is all that I have
And the life that I have
Is yours

The love that I have
Of the life that I have
Is yours and yours and yours.

A sleep I shall have
A rest I shall have

Yet death will be but a pause
For the peace of my years
In the long green grass
Will be yours and yours and yours.

*This verse, sent to me by Dr Kenneth Sinclair-Loutit, was
the individual code of the heroine of the French resistance
Violette Szabo. It was written for her – one of many poems,
apparently, that he wrote for his fellow-agents – by the chief
code-maker for Special Operations Executive, Leo Marks.*

*When I had a drink with Mr Marks on 19 February
1997, he told me that it had actually been written for an
earlier love of his, Ruth Hambro, who had been killed in a
plane crash in Canada. But he made no secret of the fact that
he had been in love with Violette; when he gave her the poem
and made her learn it by heart, he described it to her as 'a
simple statement of fact'.*

*He seemed reluctant to explain just how the poem was
used, but brought with him what appeared to be a silk scarf
which had been hers; on close inspection it proved to be
covered with microscopic letters. He told me that he was
writing a book, in which all would be made clear. (The book,*
Between Silk and Cyanide, *has since been published and I
have read it, but still don't altogether understand.)*

*When Violette Szabo was dropped into France on the
night of 6–7 June 1944 she was almost immediately taken
prisoner, though only after providing covering fire for her*

companion who got away. She survived in Nazi hands until well after the liberation of France, but was shot in Ravensbruck on 26 January 1945 by SS Scharführer Schwartzhuber, who was later hanged. She was awarded a posthumous George Cross.

~

From Stanley R. Sims, 'Sir Wilfred Grenfell: An Athletic Missionary', British Medical Journal, *19–26 December 1992:*

Grenfell was phenomenally fit. In middle life, after trudging 45 km in one day with a backpack, he ran another eight to amputate a shattered leg, helped by two assistants, one of whom fainted. He proved the equal of the explorer Bob Bartlett on a hunting expedition, and enlarged an ice hole made for fishing to have a swim. Before they parted company he extracted Bartlett's tonsils, holding him against a shed wall.

In 1908 Grenfell nearly perished when he took his dog team, against advice, across Hare Bay in a short cut to an urgent case. The ice broke up and he drifted seawards on a floe. He had to kill three dogs and wrap himself in their skins to survive the night and then use their frozen legs to make a flag pole for waving his shirt. He was rescued by five oarsmen at great personal risk.

The next year, at the age of forty-four, on his way from Liverpool to New York on the *Mauretania*, he proposed to a girl twenty years younger, after a three-day acquaintance. On being reminded that he did not even know her name, he replied that he was only interested in what it was going to be . . .

His selfless sincerity and irrepressible sense of humour won him unyielding affection, but his application of the principle 'start something, someone else will finish it' could make him an exasperating colleague . . .

~

The Roman Centurion's Song
(Roman Occupation of Britain, AD 300)

Legate, I heard the news last night – my cohort ordered
    home
By ships to Portus Itius and thence by road to Rome.
I've marched the companies aboard, the arms are
    stowed below:
Now let another take my sword. Command me not to
    go!

I've served in Britain forty years, from Vectis to the
    Wall,
I have none other home than this, nor any life at all.

Last night I did not understand, but, now the hour
draws near
That calls me to my native land, I feel that land is here.

Here where men say my name was made, here where
my work was done;
Here where my dearest dead are laid – my wife – my
wife and son;
Here where time, custom, grief and toil, age, memory,
service, love,
Have rooted me in British soil. Ah, how can I remove?

For me this land, that sea, these airs, those folk and
fields suffice.
What purple Southern pomp can match our changeful
Northern skies,
Black with December snows unshed or pearled with
August haze –
The clanging arch of steel-grey March, or June's long-
lighted days?

You'll follow widening Rhodanus till vine and olive
lean
Aslant before the sunny breeze that sweeps Nemausus
clean
To Arelate's triple gate; but let me linger on,
Here where our stiff-necked British oaks confront
Euroclydon!

You'll take the old Aurelian Road through shore-
    descending pines
Where, blue as any peacock's neck, the Tyrrhene
    Ocean shines.
You'll go where laurel crowns are won, but – will you
    e'er forget
The scent of hawthorn in the sun, or bracken in the wet?

Let me work here for Britain's sake – at any task you
    will –
A marsh to drain, a road to make or native troops to drill.
Some Western camp (I know the Pict) or granite
    Border keep,
Mid seas of heather derelict, where our old messmates
    sleep.

Legate, I come to you in tears – My cohort ordered
    home!
I've served in Britain forty years. What should I do in
    Rome?
Here is my heart, my soul, my mind – the only life I
    know.
I cannot leave it all behind. Command me not to go!

Rudyard Kipling

Rhodanus: the Rhône   *Nemausus:* Nîmes

Arelate: Arles   *Euroclydon:* 'a tempestuous wind' (*Acts*, xxvii, 14)

The transcript of a radio conversation between USS Lincoln and the Canadian authorities off the coast of Newfoundland has been widely published, with slight variations:

AUTHORITIES: Please divert your course 15 degrees to the south to avoid a collision.

LINCOLN: Recommend you divert *your* course 15 degrees to the north to avoid a collision.

AUTHORITIES: Negative. You will have to divert your course 15 degrees to the south to avert collision.

LINCOLN: This is the Captain of the US Navy ship. I say again, divert YOUR course.

AUTHORITIES: No. I say again, divert YOUR course.

LINCOLN: THIS IS THE AIRCRAFT CARRIER USS LINCOLN, THE SECOND LARGEST SHIP IN THE UNITED STATES ATLANTIC FLEET. WE ARE ACCOMPANIED BY THREE DESTROYERS, THREE CRUISERS AND NUMEROUS ESCORT VESSELS. I DEMAND THAT YOU CHANGE YOUR COURSE 15 DEGREES NORTH. I SAY AGAIN, THAT IS ONE FIVE DEGREES NORTH, OR COUNTER-MEASURES WILL BE TAKEN TO ENSURE THE SAFETY OF THIS SHIP.

AUTHORITIES: This is a lighthouse. Your call.

From an obituary notice in the Daily Telegraph, *19 December 2001:*

Melvin Burkhart, who has died aged 94, was a fairground sideshow performer known as the Human Blockhead because of his ability to drive a five-inch nail or an icepick into his head without flinching.

The Human Blockhead worked under a number of alternative titles, depending on which of his extraordinary repertoire of physical contortions he happened to be performing at the time.

As the Anatomical Wonder, he could inflate one lung at a time and dislocate his shoulders; as the Man without a Stomach, he could suck his stomach back to his spine; as the Two-Faced Man, he could frown with half his face and smile with the other half. Among many other accomplishments, he swallowed swords, threw knives and ate fire.

He was universally admired by his fellow performers, one of whom observed: 'Anyone who has ever hammered a five-inch nail into his nose owes a large debt to Melvin Burkhart.'

~

A thought on returning to the capital from a journey through Orissa, north-east India:

> I fear that some parts of Old Delhi
> Are – let's face it – a weeny bit smelhi;
>   For the rest, it's chaotic
>   But rather exotic –
> And just like you see on the telhi.

~

From the Daily Telegraph, *28 December 1992:*

Sir,

I was interested to read (letter, December 22) that Lord Delaval Beresford died in a train collision in 1906, since his uncle, the 3rd Marquess of Waterford, once proposed to one of the first railway companies in Ireland that it should start two engines in opposite directions on the same line in order that he might witness the smash. His Lordship was, I understand, prepared to pay for his pleasure.

Among his other eccentricities, he painted the Melton Mowbray toll bar red (was this the origin of the expression 'painting the town red'?), put aniseed on the hooves of a parson's horse before hunting the terrified

divine, and placed a donkey in the bed of a hapless traveller at an inn.

As for Lord Delaval's brother, Admiral Lord
Charles Beresford, whom your correspondent also
mentions, 'Charlie B.' had a hunt in full cry tattooed
down his back, with the fox going to earth in the appropriate aperture.

Lest it be thought, however, that this fine Irish sporting dynasty were too wild for their own good, another
brother, Lord William Beresford, won the VC in the
Zulu Wars.

Thomas Byrne
Dublin

*Tattoos are always good for a laugh. Judith Flanders has
called my attention to a letter from Sir Edward Burne-Jones
to Helen Mary Gaskell, 4 September 1894:*

The lady whose shoulders are tattooed with the Last
Supper is in town – at the Aquarium – and I am going
with Luke Fildes to see her. On Saturday he saw her –
the tattoos are still perfect – only she is somewhat fatter,
and all the faces of the Apostles are a little wider, and
have a tendency to smile.

My dear son Jason has thoughtfully provided me with the following list of condom flavours currently available on platform 1 of the railway station in Lady Thatcher's home town of Grantham, Lincolnshire:

Strawberries and Cream
Ice Cream
Lemon and Lime
Banana
Liquorice
Champagne
Whisky
Curry
Lager
Chocdoms
Humpy Birthday
Tropical Nights
Lads' Night Out
Kangaroo

~

Outside of a dog, a book is man's best friend. Inside of a dog, it's too dark to read.

Groucho Marx

My friend Bob Guthrie has sent me the following extracts from an American parish magazine, culled over a number of years:

Remember in prayer the many who are sick of our church and community.

The rosebud on the altar this morning is to announce the birth of David Alan Belzer, the sin of Rev. and Mrs Julius Belzer.

Tuesday at 4 p.m. there will be an ice cream social. All ladies giving milk will please come early.

Wednesday, the Ladies' Liturgy Society will meet. Mrs Jones will sing 'Put Me in My Little Bed', accompanied by the Pastor.

Thursday at 5 p.m. there will be a meeting of the Little Mothers' Club. All wishing to become little mothers, please see the Minister in his study.

This being Easter Sunday, we will ask Mrs Lewis to come forward and lay an egg on the altar.

The service will close with 'Little Drops of Water'. One of the ladies will start quietly and the rest of the congregation will join in.

Next Sunday a special collection will be taken to defray the cost of the new carpet. All those wishing to do something on the new carpet will come forward and do so.

A bean supper will be held on Tuesday evening in the church hall. Music will follow.

The ladies of the church have cast off clothing of every kind and they may be seen in the church basement Friday.

At the evening service tonight, the sermon topic will be 'What is Hell?' Come early and listen to our choir practice.

~

Be comforted, little dog; thou too at the resurrection shalt have a little golden tail.

Martin Luther

2010—2018

Dear Sir,

I like words. I like fat, buttery words, such as ooze, turpitude, glutinous, toady. I like solemn, angular, creaky words, such as straitlaced, cantankerous, pernicious, valedictory. I like spurious, black-is-white words, such as mortician, liquidate, tonsorial, demi-monde. I like suave, V-words, such as Svengali, svelte, bravura, verve. I like crunchy, brittle, crackly words, such as splinter, grapple, jostle, crusty. I like sullen, crabbed, scowling words, such as skulk, glower, scabby, churl. I like Oh-heavens, my-gracious, land's-sake words, such as tricksy, tucker, genteel, horrid. I like elegant, flowery words, such as estivate, peregrinate, Elysium, halcyon. I like wormy, squirmy, mealy words, such as crawl, blubber, squeal, drip. I like sniggly, chuckling words, such as cowlick, gurgle, bubble and burp.

I like the word screenwriter better than copywriter, so I decided to quit my job in a New York advertising agency and try my luck in Hollywood, but before taking the plunge I went to Europe for a year of study, contemplation and horsing around.

I have just returned and I still like words. May I have a few with you?

This letter was written in 1934 by a certain Robert Pirosh, and sent to as many producers, directors and studio executives as he could find. He got a job at MGM, and was later to win both an Academy Award and a Golden Globe.

~

Joseph Addison's Grand Tour of Europe began anything but auspiciously, when he slipped on his arrival at Calais and narrowly escaped drowning. He wrote to his friend William Congreve:

Paris
August 1699

Since I had the happiness to see you last I have encountered as many misfortunes as a Knight Errant. I had a fall into the water at Callice and since that several Bruises upon the Land, lame post-horses by Day and hard Beds at night, with many other dismal adventures . . . My arrival at Paris was at first no less uncomfortable where I could not see a face nor hear a Word that I have ever met with before: so that my most agreeable companions have bin statues and Pictures wch are many of 'em very extraordinary but what

particularly recommends 'em is that they don't Speak
French and they have a very good quality, rarely to be met
with in this Country of not being too Talkative.

~

Yet if His Majesty, our Sovereign Lord
   Should, of his own accord,
   Friendly himself invite
And say, 'I'll be your guest tomorrow night',
How should we stir ourselves, call and command
All hands to work! 'Let no man idle stand.

'Set me fine Spanish tables in the hall.
   See they be fitted all;
   Let there be room to eat
And order taken that there want no meat.
See every sconce and candlestick made bright
That without tapers they may give a light.

'Look to the presence; are the carpets spread?
   The dazie o'er the head,
   The cushions in the chairs,
And all the candles lighted on the stairs?
Perfume the chambers, and in any case
Let each man give attendance in his place.'

Thus, if the King were coming, would we do,
　　And 'twere good reason too;
　　For 'tis a duteous thing
To show all honour to an earthly king,
And after all our travail and our cost,
So he be pleas'd, to think no labour lost.

But at the coming of the King of Heaven
　　All's set at six and seven;
　　We wallow in our sin,
Christ cannot find a chamber in the inn.
We entertain Him always like a stranger
And, as at first, still lodge him in a manger.

I have loved this poem all my life. It was discovered, unsigned, in the Library of Christ Church, Oxford, and is generally labelled anonymous. Recently attempts have been made to attribute it to Thomas Ford (1580–1648), but Ford was a composer – rather a good one – and none of the few scraps of verse that he left can hold a candle to this.

~

If you imagine the 4,500 million years of Earth's history compressed into a normal earthly day, then life begins very early, about 4 a.m., with the rise of the first simple, single-celled organisms, but then advances no further for the next sixteen hours. Not until almost eight-thirty in the evening, with the day five-sixths over, has the Earth anything to show the universe but a restless skin of microbes. Then, finally, the first sea plants appear, followed twenty minutes later by the first jellyfish . . . At 9.04 p.m., trilobites swim on to the scene . . . Just before 10 p.m. plants begin to pop up on the land. Soon after, with less than two hours left in the day, the first land creatures follow.

Thanks to ten minutes or so of balmy weather, by 10.24 the Earth is covered in the great carboniferous forests whose residues give us all our coal, and the first winged insects are evident. Dinosaurs plod on to the scene just before 11 p.m. and hold sway for about three-quarters of an hour. At twenty-one minutes to midnight they vanish and the age of mammals begins. Humans emerge one minute and seventeen seconds before midnight. The whole of our recorded history, on this scale, would be no more than a few seconds, a single human lifetime barely an instant . . .

Perhaps an even more effective way of grasping our extreme recentness as part of this 4.5-billion-year-old picture is to stretch your arms to their fullest extent and imagine that width as the entire history of the Earth. On this scale, according to John McPhee in *Basin and Range*, the distance from the fingertips of one hand to the wrist of the other is Pre-Cambrian. All of complex life is in one hand, 'and in a single stroke with a medium-grained nail file you could eradicate human history'.

Bill Bryson, *A Short History of Nearly Everything*

~

In the 1930s, when C. A. Alington was Head Master of Eton, Jo Grimond, later Leader of the Liberal Party but then President of the Eton Political Society, asked Mahatma Gandhi down to speak. William Douglas-Home remembered:

Gandhi had that girlfriend of his, Miss Slade, with him. They came back to the Head Master's house where they were staying and Mr Gandhi went to bed because he said he was tired after his talk. And when Mrs Alington went to bed half an hour later, there on the mat outside Gandhi's door was Miss Slade, lying under a blanket with a pillow. Mrs Alington said, 'Go to your room, Miss Slade.' And Miss Slade said, 'But I've slept outside the dear Mahatma's door for the last seven years, every night,' to which Mrs Alington replied, 'Not while I'm President of the Women's Institutes you don't,' and made her get up and put her into her bedroom and locked the door.

Eric Anderson and Adam Nicolson, *About Eton*

You do not seem to have the zest for life that I had at your age. However, if you keep your elbows off the table and read Sir Walter Scott, the rest may come.

These wise words were written by Lady Frances Balfour, fifth daughter of the eighth Duke of Argyll, to her seventeen-year-old daughter, Frances Dugdale.

Lady Frances, who was born in 1858 and died in 1931, was the sister-in-law of A. J. Balfour, the Prime Minister, and an ardent champion of women's suffrage. Apart from five biographies, she also published a two-volume autobiography entitled Ne Obliviscaris: Dinna Forget.

~

I feel that before I die I must note down the only conversation I ever had with Margaret Thatcher. It must have been in 1979 or 1980, while I was a member of the board of the English National Opera. The Prime Minister had not been very long in office when we invited her and her husband to a performance of *Tosca*. When it was over there was a little reception, in the course of which I went up to her and said I hoped she had enjoyed it. 'Oh yes,' she said, and then, to my astonishment, lectured to me about *Tosca* for several minutes: where it belonged in Puccini's works, who had been the greatest singers of note, and much else besides. I realised that, typically, she had sent for a brief, and learnt it. (She could never bear to be seen at a disadvantage.) The lecture finished and me still there, she had to find another superiority – clothes.

PM: Of course, if one had been producing it oneself, one would have made certain changes.

JJN: Oh really, Prime Minister, what changes for example?

PM: Well, I mean, Tosca's fichu.

JJN: But, Prime Minister, what was wrong with Tosca's fichu?

PM: The colour, of course.

JJN: Well, it was red.

PM: Yes, it was *red*!

JJN: But, Prime Minister, what colour should Tosca's fichu have been?

PM: Cerise.

~

The Hedg-hog

When he findeth Apples or Grapes on the earth, hee rowleth himselfe upon them, until he have filled all his prickles, so foorth he goeth, making a noyse like a cart wheele.

Edward Topsell, *History of Four Footed Beasts*, 1607

*General Freiherr Kurt von Hammerstein-Equord (1878–1943) was Chief of the German High Command. He supervised the manual on the Military Unit Command (*Truppenführung*), which was published in October 1933. Here is an extract:*

I divide my officers into four classes; the clever, the lazy, the industrious and the stupid. Each officer possesses at least two of these qualities. Those who are clever and industrious I appoint to the General Staff. Use can be made in certain circumstances of those who are stupid and lazy. The man who is clever and lazy qualifies for the highest command. He has the requisite nerves and the mental clarity to deal with all situations. But whoever is stupid and industrious must be got rid of, for he is too dangerous.

~

When my daughter Artemis was researching her dazzling biography of Paddy Leigh Fermor in his house at Kardamyli she went through his files and came across the following:

Detached Oddments
Not Very Important Oddments
Own Oddments
Own Unsorted Oddments

Unsorted but Interesting
Oldish – Needs Sorting
Badly Needs Sorting
Current: Unsorted
Current: Various
Vol III: Odds and Ends
Crete: Mixed Bag
Tiring Duplicates
Disjecta Membra
Scattered Intractables
Official Bumph
Flotsam

~

To mark the anniversary of Waterloo comes this extract from the biography of the Duke of Wellington by Elizabeth Longford, kindly sent to me by her daughter Antonia:

Wellington on 13 June was still waiting for the incontrovertible sign that Napoleon had marched. Everything, apart from that essential knowledge, was ready. He had even received from his boot-maker, Hoby, two pairs of 'Wellington' boots specially ordered for the campaign to replace a modified half-boot which did not quite come up to Wellington's developing ideas on the subject.

Bruxelles
April 11th 1815

Mr Hoby

The last boots you sent me were still too small in the calf of the leg & about an inch and a half too short in the leg. Send me two pairs more, altered as I have above described.

Your most faithful Servt.
Wellington

The great Mr Hoby of St James's Street prided himself not only on his boots but also on his preaching – at a Methodist chapel in Islington. On hearing the news of the British rout of the French at Vitoria he is said to have remarked complacently:

If Lord Wellington had any other boot-maker than myself, he never would have had his great and constant successes; for my boots and prayers bring his Lordship out of all his difficulties.

~

There's a lovely little poem by Noel Coward which I had quite forgotten until Patricia Hodge kindly reminded me of it:

When I have fears, as Keats had fears,
Of the moment I'll cease to be,
I console myself with vanished years,
Remembered laughter, remembered tears,
And the peace of the changing sea.

When I feel sad, as Keats felt sad,
That my life is so nearly done,
It gives me comfort to dwell upon
Remembered friends who are dead and gone
And the jokes we had, and the fun.

How happy they are I cannot know,
But happy am I who loved them so.

~

Details of the forthcoming trip to the BBC were circulated and members told not to bring sharp or pointed items such as knives, razor blades, cutlery, nail files, scissors, penknives, de-activated firearms, ammunition, pepper spray or CS gas, all of which was duly noted.

From a report to the Bradfield Women's Institute, 2015

Lieutenant-General Sir Adrian Carton de Wiart VC, KBE, CB, CMG, DSO (1880–1963), was according to Wikipedia, 'A British army officer of Belgian and Irish descent. He served in the Boer War, First World War and Second World War; was shot in the face, head, hand, stomach, ankle, leg, hip and ear; survived two plane crashes; tunnelled out of a POW camp; and pulled off his own fingers when the doctor refused to amputate them.' He lost an eye and a hand. He is thought to have been the model for Brigadier Ritchie-Hook in Evelyn Waugh's Sword of Honour *trilogy. Hugo Vickers has kindly sent me a copy of his autobiography,* Happy Odyssey. *It is excessively modest, mentioning none of his decorations – nor his two (successive) wives and two daughters; but in other respects it is rich indeed.*

I was very keen on racing, and in Cairo was offered a mount in a hurdle race, but it entailed my taking off seven pounds in weight in twenty-four hours. Turkish baths were inadequate, so I wrapped myself up in countless sweaters topped by an overcoat, practically ran the six or seven miles to the Pyramids, climbed them and staggered back again. Alas, although I lost the required seven pounds, I reduced myself to such a state of collapse that I had a bad fall in the race, severe concussion, and did not ride again that winter . . .

Parlour tricks were compulsory, and my ability to tear a pack of cards in half . . . earned me a steady income, but the Almighty must have resented my ill-gotten gains for, later, he removed one of my hands. Another rather showy trick of mine was to dive over four men and be caught the other side by a couple of fielders . . . One night the fielders forgot their jobs and I landed on my shoulder without hurting myself. I continued ever after to perform this trick unaided. The third trick, which lasted me well until last year I fractured my spine, was to straddle a chair and fall over backwards . . . Beyond one occasion when an officer's spur finished its course up another officer's nose, I cannot recollect any real disasters.

One day, the general was asked to second a friend in a duel:

I agreed at once, as I think duelling is a most excellent solution in matters of the heart, and saw that my man was a tremendous fire-eater with only one object in view, to kill his opponent . . . I went off to see his opponent, whom I knew; true to form, he found the whole idea quite ridiculous. I assured him that my friend was adamant and determined to fight – preferably with pistols at the range of a few feet . . . As a last resort our opponent produced what he considered a telling argument, which was that if this episode was found out we should all get into serious trouble . . . My reply was that the war was on, everyone too busy to be interested, and that it would be simple to go to some secluded spot like Ashdown Forest with a can of petrol and cremate the remains of whichever was killed. This suggestion finished him off . . . It seemed to me that as he did not like the lady enough to fight for her, he needed a thrashing.

~

In a previous Cracker *I included an extract from a letter to Nancy Mitford from her sister Diana: 'When his aunt died aged 88, his mother, who was 90, only said "Elle a toujours été fragile" and didn't care a bit.' The following is quoted from the correspondence of Mr Justice Holmes and Harold J. Laski:*

I must not forget to tell you of the death of a Fellow of Trinity College aged ninety-seven. His funeral was attended by a brother of ninety-nine. The latter was much distressed and said he had always told his junior that theological research was not compatible with longevity. 'God', he solemnly told Rutherford, 'does not mean us to pry into these matters.' After the funeral the old man went back to Trinity and solemnly drank his half-bottle of port. He was asked his prescription for health and said with great fervour, 'Never deny yourself anything.' He explained that he had never married as he found fidelity restricting as a young man. 'I was once engaged when I was forty,' he said, 'and I found it gave me very serious constipation. So I broke off the engagement and the lady quite understood.' He was very anxious not to be thought past the age of flirtation.

~

I have many times asked myself, not without wonder, the source of a certain error which, since it is committed by all the old without exception, can be believed to be proper and natural to man: namely, that they all praise the past and blame the present, revile our actions and behaviour and everything which they themselves did not do when they were young, and affirm, too, that every good custom and way of life, every virtue and, in short, all things imaginable are always going from bad to worse. And truly it seems against all reason and a cause for astonishment that maturity of age, which, with its long experience, in all other respects usually perfects a man's judgement, in this matter corrupts it so much that he does not realise that, if the world were always growing worse and if fathers were generally better than their sons, we would long since have become so rotten that no further deterioration would be possible.

Baldassare Castiglione (1478–1529), *The Book of the Courtier*

~

In June 1882, John Ruskin was taken to a performance of Die Meistersinger. This proved a mistake. On the 30th, he wrote to his friend Mrs Burne-Jones:

Of all the *bête*, clumsy, blundering, boggling, baboon-blooded stuff I ever saw on a human stage, that thing last night beat [everything] – as far as the story and acting went; and of all the affected, sapless, soulless, beginning-less, endless, topless, bottomless, topsiturveyest, tongs-and-boniest [*sic*] doggerel of sounds I ever endured the deadliness of, that eternity of nothing was the deadliest – as far as the sound went. I never was so relieved, so far as I can remember in my life, by the stopping of any sound – not excepting railway whistles – as I was by the cessation of the cobbler's bellowing, even the serenader's caricature twangle was a rest after it. As for the great *Lied*, I never made out where it began, or where it ended – except by the fellow's coming off the block.

Which reminds me that a number of previous Crackers *have noted severe critical misjudgements. Here is another one from* Isis, *17 November 1928:*

Through about seventy lines Mr Auden continues to show his inability to appreciate the meaning of words.

And John Betjeman loved to recall the remark of the archi-
tect H. S. Goodhart-Rendel to Osbert Lancaster on his first
visit to the Parthenon. After gazing at it in silence for a
considerable time, he at last gave his opinion:

> Well, not what you'd call
> an *unqualified* success, is it?

~

Thanks to my sister-in-law Virginia Shapiro here is a poem
on the terrible loss of memory that comes with age, from the
book Questions About Angels *by the American poet Billy*
Collins:

Forgetfulness

The name of the author is the first to go,
Followed obediently by the title, the plot,
The heartbreaking conclusion, the entire novel
Which suddenly becomes one you have never read,
Never even heard of.

As if, one by one, the memories you used to harbor
Decided to retire to the southern hemisphere of the
   brain,
To a little fishing village where there are no phones.

Long ago you kissed the names of the nine Muses
    goodbye
And watched the quadratic equation pack its bag,
And even now as you memorize the order of the planets,

Something else is slipping away, a state flower perhaps,
The address of an uncle, the capital of Paraguay.

Whatever it is you are struggling to remember,
It is not poised on the tip of your tongue,
Not even lurking in some obscure corner of your spleen.

It has floated away down a dark mythological river
Whose name begins with an L as far as you can recall,
Well on your own way to oblivion where you will join
    those
Who have even forgotten how to swim and how to ride
    a bicycle.

No wonder you rise in the middle of the night
To look up the date of a famous battle in a book on war.
No wonder the moon in the window seems to have
    drifted
Out of a love poem that you used to know by heart.

~

My friend Julius Drake sends me this little gem. It comes from a letter written by Anton Chekhov to his friend Alexei Suvorin on 26 October 1895:

Tolstoy's daughters are very nice. They adore their father and have a fanatic faith in him. That is a sure sign that Tolstoy is indeed a mighty moral force, for if he were insincere and not above reproach the first to regard him sceptically would be his daughters, because daughters are shrewd creatures and you can't pull the wool over their eyes. You can fool a fiancée or a mistress as much as you please, and in the eyes of a loving woman even a donkey may pass for a philosopher, but daughters are another matter.

~

On 1 November 1995 Christie's New York held a sale of Boldini portraits, one of which depicted the famous Marchesa Luisa Casati (1881–1957). The catalogue recounts that she also sat for a bronze by Jacob Epstein, who had the following story to tell:

The Marchesa arrived in a taxi-cab at ten o'clock (in the morning) and left it waiting for her. We began the sittings, and her Medusa-like head kept me busy until nightfall. It was snowing outside, and a report came in that the taxi man had at length made a declaration. He did not care if it was Epstein or if it was a countess; he would not wait any longer. On hearing this Casati shouted: 'He is a Bolshevik! Ask him to wait a little longer.' He was given tea and a place by the fire and shown the bookshelf.

The winter light had failed, and I had many candles brought in. They formed a circle round my weird sitter, with the fire in the grate piled high to give more light. The tireless Marchesa, with her over-large blue-veined eyes, sat with a basilisk stare; and as if to bear out her epithet of 'Bolshevik', the taxi man picked out for himself *The Brothers Karamazov* to read and ceased to protest.

The Medusa-like mask was finished the next day.

Those huge eyes were, we are informed, 'later to be outlined not only with black eye-paint but with strips of black velvet which she glued to her eyelids'.

~

Of all the countless comparisons which have been made between Gladstone and Disraeli, the best for me is by Winston Churchill's mother, Jennie Jerome:

When I left the dining room after sitting next to Gladstone, I thought he was the cleverest man in England. But when I sat next to Disraeli, I left feeling that I was the cleverest woman.

And here is Ellen Wilkinson, member of the coalition cabinet during the Second World War:

When Mr Attlee is presiding in the absence of the Prime Minister, the Cabinet meets on time, goes systematically through its agenda, makes the necessary decisions, and goes home after three or four hours' work. When Mr Churchill presides we never reach the agenda and we decide nothing. But we go home to bed at midnight, conscious of having been present at an historic occasion.

From Kingsley Martin, *Harold Laski*

Or, as Churchill himself confessed:

All I wanted was compliance with my wishes after reasonable discussion.

The Second World War: The Hinge of Fate

∼

The usual limericks. The first is by Dylan Thomas, a remarkable summing-up of the Christian religion:

> There was an old bugger called God,
> Who put a young virgin in pod:
>   This amazing behaviour
>   Produced Christ our saviour,
> Who died on a cross, poor old sod.

And the only mathematical limerick I know:

$$\frac{12 + 144 + 20 + 3\sqrt{4}}{7} + (5 \times 11) = 9^2 + 0$$

which is, when translated:

> A dozen, a gross and a score,
> Plus three times the square root of four,
>   Divided by seven,
>   Plus five times eleven,
> Is nine squared – and not a bit more.

~

Here, considerably abridged, is The Times *obituary of the Rev. Brian Brindley, who died on 1 August 2001, aged sixty-nine:*

Not since Father Hope Patten contrived to die surrounded by bishops visiting Walsingham during a Lambeth Conference could a clerical death have been better choreographed. Brian Brindley, larger-than-life *bon viveur*, former Church of England priest and Canon of Christ Church, died of a heart attack between the dressed crab and the *boeuf en croûte* at a party at the Athenaeum to celebrate his seventieth birthday. It could hardly have been more appropriate, for this colourful character loved food and loved company, especially when he was the centre of attention . . .

Brian Frederick Brindley (to which he added as confirmation names Dominick and Titus) was born in London. After the Low Church tradition of his school, Stowe, going up to Oxford in 1951, with its rich supermarket of Anglo-Catholic worship, must have been heaven for him. His fellow under-graduates elected him President of the Junior Common Room, and the JCR book records a suggestion for the floodlighting of the delicate French Gothic spire of Exeter College Chapel and Brindley's reply: 'Suggestion noted, but though the spirit is willing the *flèche* is weak.'

After training for the priesthood at Ely Theological College . . . within four years this gifted and ambitious young priest was appointed vicar of the unprepossessing church and parish of Holy Trinity, Oxford Road, Reading. Bishop Harry Carpenter said he had put the most impossible priest in the most impossible parish.

Immediately the services began to be advertised in the *Church Times* with the helpful information 'Fast Trains from Paddington'. Many, indeed, did take the fast train, and not only from Paddington, for he turned 'HTR' – as it became known – into an eclectic shrine where the more obscure festivals of the Church could be guaranteed to be observed with more ceremony than perhaps anywhere else in the world. Through clouds of incense a liturgical *son et lumière* was performed, highlighting the elevated host, the reliquaries and the pulpit at dramatic points during the service.

At a time when continental Catholics were disposing of vestments, Brindley could be found sniffing around the *marchés aux puces* in Paris, rescuing often priceless chasubles to be brought back for use in Reading. He salvaged the splendid Pugin screen from Birmingham's Roman Catholic cathedral and installed it in his church. Wherever there was an ecclesiastical 'high do' Brindley was to be found, sporting ever more extraordinary outfits, from cottas embroidered with cauliflowers and bananas to albs consisting almost entirely of lace. The ensemble would be topped by a Spanish biretta or *cappello Romano*. To be invited to a party at the Reading presbytery was like passing through a junk shop of exaggerated bad taste . . .

He used his calligraphic and artistic skills month by month as he personally produced *The Battle*, his parish magazine (named after the district in Reading that

comprised his parish, rather than the ecclesiastical contro-
versy on which he flourished). Its Gothic cover and other
illustrations were all the work of the multi-talented vicar,
and it had a circulation far wider than his flock, with
postal subscribers throughout the country, and indeed
the world. Consistent Christian teaching was accompanied by articles on art, cookery, embroidery, heraldry . . .

His home at Brighton, decorated and furnished in the
same inflated Baroque as his vicarage in Reading, continued to be a venue for his love of entertaining and food.

~

Good days are to be gathered like sunshine in grapes, to
be trodden and bottled into wine and kept for age to sip
at ease beside the fire. If the traveller has vintaged well
he need trouble to wander no longer; the ruby moments
glow in his glass at will.

Freya Stark

~

On the 28th day of November
Outside the house of Macroom,
The Tans in their big Crossley tenders
Were hurtlin' along to their doom.

But the boys of the column were waiting,
With their hand-grenades primed on the spot
And the Irish Republican Army
Made shite of the whole fockin' lot.

IRA song from 1916

~

I was delighted to learn – from Eric Hobsbawm's essay
'Art and Power' – that the subject set for Italy's Premio
Carmona painting competition in 1939 was 'Listening to
a Speech by Il Duce on the Radio'.

~

*The execution of Mary Queen of Scots took place at
Fotheringhay Castle on 8 February 1587. It inspired the
Jesuit martyr Robert Southwell to write a wonderful poem:*

The pounded spice both tast and sent doth please:
In fadinge smoke the force doth incense showe;
The perisht kernel springeth with increase;
The lopped tree doth best and soonest growe.

God's spice I was, and poundinge was my due;
In fadinge breath my incense savoured best;

Death was the meane my kernel to renewe;
By loppinge shott I up to heavenly rest.

Some thinges more perfit are in their decaye,
Like sparke that going out geeves clerest light;
Such was my happe, whose doleful dying daye
Began my joye and termed fortune's spight.

Alive a Queene, now dead I am a Saint;
Once *Mary* cald, my name now Martyr is;
From earthly reigne debarred by restrainte,
In liew whereof I raigne in heavenly blisse.

My life, my griefe, my death, hath wrought my joye;
My freendes, my foyle, my foes, my weale procurd,
My speedie death hath shortned long annoye,
And losse of life an endles life assurd.

My scaffolde was the bedd where ease I founde;
The blocke a pillowe of eternall rest.
My headman cast mee in blesfull swounde;
His axe cutt of my cares from comb red brest.

Rue not my death, rejoyce at my repose;
It was no death to mee but to my woe,
The budd was opened to let owt the rose,
The cheynes unloosed to let the captive goe.

A Prince by birth, a prisoner by mishappe,
From crowne to crosse, from throne to thrall I fell.
My right my ruth, my tytles wrought my trappe;
My weale my woe, my worldly heaven my hell.

By death from prisoner to a prince enhaunced;
From crosse to crowne, from thrall to throne againe,
My ruth my right, my trappe my styll advanced
Frome woe to weale, from hell to heavenly raigne.

*Just eight years later – after ten sessions in the torture cham-
ber – Southwell was hanged, drawn and quartered at
Tyburn. He was canonised in 1970.*

~

*I must have started hundreds – literally – of lectures on
Venice with the story of Robert Benchley, on his first arrival
in Venice, sending a telegram to Harold Ross, editor of the*
New Yorker, *with the words 'Streets full of water please
advise'. I was therefore amused to see it quoted by Gyles
Brandreth in the* Oldie *of April 2018, together with another,
which was new to me. This, he writes,*

. . . was said by the great American film director Billy
Wilder, in the mid-1950s when he was in Paris making a

movie. It was at the time when the bidet was coming into fashion in the US as a must-have bathroom accessory, and the then Mrs Wilder, back in Los Angeles, wanted to have one. She instructed her husband to buy a bidet while he was filming in France and have it shipped over to Hollywood. Unfortunately, so great had been the recent demand for bidets that, when Wilder went out in search of one, he failed to find it. He wired his wife with the news: 'Unable to find bidet suggest headstand in shower.'

~

I have always loved the sea; earlier Crackers *have included several descriptions of it. My friend Brian Young has called my attention to another, by the Irish poet George Darley (1795–1846). It comes from his 'Nepenthe', which alas he left unfinished:*

> Hurry me, Nymphs! O, hurry me
> Far above the grovelling sea,
> Which, with blind weakness and bass roar
> Casting his white age on the shore,
> Wallows along that slimy floor;
> With his widespread webbèd hands
> Seeking to climb the level sands,
> But rejected still to rave
> Alive in his uncovered grave.

A. E. Housman commented: 'The man who wrote it had seen the sea, and the man who read it sees the sea again.'

~

In early September 1959 I received a letter from my old chum Philip Ziegler. We were both in the Foreign Service; Philip was in Vientiane, I was in Beirut. The letter ran as follows:

My dear John Julius,

On Sept. 11 or so a great, grotesque lobster will trip and fall heavily from a plane at Beirut aerodrome. It will wear a monocle, and probably a kilt. It will be called Alec Brodie, will have a DSO and an MC, and will be the ex-Military Attaché in Laos and the new one in the Lebanon.

Alec first arrived in my life about three weeks before the War Office condescended to let us know that our pleas to be spared a M.A. because we had nowhere to put him were to be ignored. He telegraphed from Seoul: 'To the Assistant Military Attaché: Will be glad to take over any stores left by former M.A. But do not like Ballantyne's whisky. Brodie.' This took us aback, but we worked out who he must be and the correspondence began to work up speed. 'Following for Brodie:

There has been no M.A. Consequently there is no
A.M.A. and no whisky. When do you arrive?' 'To the
A.M.A.: Then I will bring my own whisky. Did the
M.A. have a dog which I should take on? Brodie.'
'There was no M.A. Consequently no A.M.A. and no
dog. When do you arrive?' 'To the A.M.A.: I am glad
the M.A. had no dog. I do not like dogs. Should I bring
a) tent, b) jeep, c) chauffeur, d) clerk, e) officer's
servant, f) canvas bucket? Brodie.' 'There is no A.M.A.
Tent, jeep and canvas bucket will all be useful. Advise
against a) chauffeur, b) clerk and c) officer's servant
since there is nowhere for them to live except a) tent, b)
jeep and c) canvas bucket.' 'To the A.M.A.: Thank you.
What about rope?' This was ignored and for fourteen
blissful days we tried to kid ourselves that it was all a
bad dream. Then: 'To the A.M.A.: Arrive noon tomorrow. Chauffeur, clerk, jeep, officer's servant, tent and
canvas bucket follow by road. Brodie.'

Tomorrow was today by the time we got the telegram and even before the news had sunk in he was
upon us, in a lorry commandeered from somewhere
with six cases of whisky, fourteen cases of beer and one
very small suitcase, all flown up overweight at the
expense of the War Office.

I commend Alec to you heartily, tho' with certain
reservations. If you ask him to dinner he will destroy
– not just break: crush, annihilate – your coffee-cups,
spill wine on your table and cigar-ash on your carpet,

go to sleep after dinner, wake up with a start at ten o'clock and proceed to lecture the most Lebanese of your guests in execrable but determined French on the genealogies of the greater Scottish families. I have heard him talk for half an hour without stop on the ramifications of the Frasers to the Laotian captain who had once been to France on a course and had a vague impression that Scotland was somewhere in America. But for all this his goodwill and kindness are immense, his patience and tolerance inexhaustible, he has the most unexpected and charming humility and, if the Lebanese have anything at all in common with the Laotians or Koreans, they will love him.

Be kind to him. Love, Philip

P.S. Despite his medals and great gallantry, his many wounds are all self-inflicted. Never drive with him if you can avoid it.

~

Ann Thwaite has called my attention to a nice story told by Roy Jenkins in his Lives of the Chancellors. *It concerns Sir John Simon, formerly both Chancellor of the Exchequer and Lord Chancellor, and the Oxford left-wing economist G. D. H. Cole:*

Returning from a weekend [at All Souls] on a Monday morning, Simon encountered Cole on the platform of Oxford station and greeted him with his well-known false bonhomie. As the London train came in Cole, disapproving of Simon and eager to make a display of semi-proletarianism as well as to escape, said 'I must get along to my third-class compartment' and disappeared down the platform. Simon, determined not to be frustrated in his search for ecumenical companionship, announced that he always travelled 'third' himself and loped after him. In those days railway tickets were neat little cardboard rectangles about two inches by one, first-class ones virginally white, third-class ones more earthly green. When the ticket-collector came round they both, with varying degrees of embarrassment, produced white tickets.

~

I have always been delighted at the prospect of a new day, a fresh try, one more start, with perhaps a bit of magic waiting somewhere behind the morning.

J. B. Priestley

~

Not my vegetarian dinner, not my lime juice
  minus gin,
Quite can drown a faint conviction that we may
  be born in sin.

John Betjeman

~

There was a surreal conversation yesterday between the official Twitter accounts of St Paul's and Canterbury Cathedral. 'Is it true that you have Saint Bartholomew's left arm?' St Paul's asked. 'Not sure,' Canterbury replied, 'we did have St Swithun's head, but it was lost in a Viking raid.' After digging in the crypt, Canterbury came back. Yes, St Bart's arm (or so an archbishop claimed it to be) was donated in 1023. It also had relics of St Dunstan and St Alphage. Not fair, huffed St Paul's. 'But you have Wellington, Nelson, Wren etc.,' Canterbury observed. Into this updating of 'Oranges and Lemons' butted Portsmouth Cathedral. 'We have a bit of [Thomas] Becket,' they told Canterbury. 'You can't have him back.'

The Times, 26 August 2015

~

My friend Charles Swallow tells me of a tombstone in Ripon Cathedral. It reads:

> Remember man, as thou pass by
> As thou art now, so once was I.
> As I am now, so wilt thou be;
> Prepare therefore to follow me.

Beneath these words someone – probably a choirboy – had written in chalk:

> To follow thee we'd be content
> Did we but know which way thou went.

~

At Mary Soames's memorial service, held in Westminster Abbey on 20 November 2014, Richard Eyre read these few lines from David Hare's play Racing Demon:

I love that bit where the plane begins to climb, the ground smoothes away behind you, the buildings, the hills. Then the white patches. The vision gets bleary. The cloud becomes a hard shelf. The land is still there. But all you see is white and the horizon.

And then you turn and head towards the sun.

This Poem

This poem is dangerous; it should not be left
Within the reach of children, or even adults
Who might swallow it whole, with possibly
Undesirable side-effects. If you come across
An unattended, unidentified poem
In a public place, do not attempt to tackle it
Yourself. Send it (preferably, in a sealed container)
To the nearest centre of learning, where it will be
   rendered
Harmless, by experts. Even the simplest poem
May destroy your immunity to human emotions.
All poems must carry a Government warning. Words
Can seriously affect your heart.

Elma Mitchell

~

At the end of the lawn there was a sundial; they looked at
it and it had got the time right. 'I'm always amazed,' said
Clelia, 'to find the sun is so reliable.'

Margaret Drabble, Jerusalem the Golden

*Hilaire Belloc was somewhat less trusting of sundials. Asked to
produce a short verse to be inscribed on a new one, he suggested:*

I am a sundial, and I make a botch
Of what is done far better by a watch.

Sam Goldwyn's comment is also worth remembering. On what seems to have been the first time he ever saw one, he was heard to murmur:

What will they think of next?

~

When the Duke of Medina Sidonia was appointed by King Philip II to the command of the Spanish Armada, he replied as follows:

My health is not equal to such a voyage, for I know by experience of the little I have been at sea that I am always seasick and always catch cold. My family is burdened with a debt of nine hundred thousand ducats, and I could not spend a rial in the King's service. Since I have had no experience either of the sea or of war, I cannot feel that I ought to command so important an enterprise. I know nothing of what the Marquis of Santa Cruz has been doing, or of what intelligence he has of England, so that I feel I should give but a bad account of myself, commanding thus blindly, and being obliged to rely on the advice of others, without knowing good from bad, or which of my advisers might want to deceive or displace me. The Adelantado Major of Castile is much fitter for this post than I. He is a man of much experience in military and naval matters, and a good Christian too.

As Garrett Mattingly writes, 'this is not exactly the spirit that conquered Mexico and Peru.' The poor Duke got the job anyway; the royal secretaries confessed that they had not dared show his letter to the King.

~

From Dryden's translation of Lucretius, De Rerum Natura*:*

When the youthful pair more closely join,
When hands in hands they lock, and thighs in thighs
    they twine,
Just in the raging foam of full desire,
When both press on, both murmur, both expire,
They grip, they squeeze, their humid tongues they
    dart,
As each would force their way to t'other's heart:
In vain; they only cruise about the coast;
For bodies cannot pierce, nor be in bodies lost;
As sure they strive to be, when both engage

In that tumultuous momentary rage.
So 'tangled in the nets of love they lie,
Till man dissolves in that excess of joy.

~

Oh how I miss Simon Barnes. For thirty-two years he was the Chief Sports Writer for The Times, *to which he also contributed a superb weekly column about wildlife. Here he is, writing from the RSPB nature reserve in Minsmere, Suffolk:*

The dawn chorus at this beautiful place is always different, but the star is always the same. It doesn't wait for dawn and sings the night away, but at dawn it always redoubles its frantic and extraordinary efforts. The nightingale's song is so passionate and glorious that it is almost too much to bear. The bird itself seems to be on the point of bursting under the strain of it, whistling higher and higher so that it could almost explode with the effort, then the throbbing jug-jug-jug drumming that could shake it apart. The nightingale is the greatest musician of them all: one study counted 250 different phrases used by a singing bird, which were based on 600 different sound units.

So much, so elaborate, so lovely: is this really just a mechanical come-hither, a peremptory biological summons to sex, a keep-out signal to opposing males? Or does the nightingale also sing for the joy of the thing itself, quite as much as for sex and competition?

It is hard to believe that any creature can give so much of itself to anything without being utterly caught up in the delight of doing, in the joy of creation. For the song is far more complex, far more lovely, than it needs to be. It refuses to be reduced to its biological function.

When I listened to the nightingales in full song in the silver-grey damp of that Minsmere morning, it seemed to me that the song was more than incidentally beautiful. It sounded as if the birds were deliberately creating something that pleased them. Dangerous ground: because in saying this I am saying that the bird is creating art, and that is supposed to be a strictly human preserve.

But human hearts and minds are stirred by the richness and variety of the nightingale's song and, no question, the hearts and minds of nightingales are stirred as well. We have more in common with the wild things than we like to think: the barriers between human beings and the other species that share this planet with us (albeit on increasingly unequal terms) are not as solid and insurmountable as we choose to pretend.

~

In 1747, Dr Samuel Johnson presented his plan for a comprehensive dictionary to Lord Chesterfield with the words:

I know that the work in which I engage is generally considered as drudgery for the blind, as the proper toil of artless industry; a task that requires neither the light of learning nor the activity of genius, but may be successfully performed without any higher quality than that of bearing burthens with dull patience and beating the track of the alphabet with sluggish resolution.

We know that later they quarrelled, Johnson believing that Chesterfield was claiming too much of the credit; he accused him of displaying 'the morals of a whore and the manners of a dancing-master'. When he came to 'patron' in the Dictionary, *his description read; 'commonly a wretch who supports with insolence and is paid with flattery'.*

~

In April 1980 Harold Macmillan went to Athens to receive a prize of some kind. Paddy Leigh Fermor wrote to Sir Aymer Maxwell:

I heard Mr Macmillan on a sofa explaining the War of Troy to some amazed Greeks: 'Of course, it was nothing to do with Helen at all. The Trojans wanted to get hold of a young Greek *filly* as their own bloodstock was probably rather poor, and sent Paris over to pinch it, which he did. That passage of the old men on the Scaean gate admiring "Helen" as she passed' – there followed a rumble of hexameters – 'has never been properly understood. Can't you see it, somebody trotting this beautiful young blood mare past – probably a chestnut with flowing mane and tail, a blaze on the brow and four white socks – she must have been charming . . .'

'But what about the wooden horse, Mr Prime Minister?' 'They've got *that* all wrong too! The Trojans were a wily and intelligent lot – they wouldn't have been fooled by such a transparent device, not for a moment. No, it must merely have been the horse-box sent to fetch the stolen steed back in. Something of that kind, don't you know . . .'

They looked very surprised.

~

This passage comes from my son-in-law Antony Beevor's superb D-Day. *He is writing of the American 5th Infantry Division, in early August 1944:*

Like the British, they too had encountered difficult hilly country and woods. It was a curious advance, with bouts of intense fighting, then moments of uneasy calm. The commander of one company described a strange experience as they advanced along a forest track. 'The woods seemed to cast an eerie spell over us as though we were the subjects of a fairy enchantment', he wrote. He and his men suddenly heard a soft, gentle clapping. 'As we came closer we could see the shadowy forms of French men and women and children, lining the roadway, not talking, some crying softly, but most just gently clapping, extending for several hundred feet on both sides of the track. A little girl came alongside me. She was blonde, pretty and maybe all of five years old. She trustingly put her hand in mine and walked a short way with me, then stopped and waved until we were out of sight.' Even fifty years later he could still hear the sound of soft clapping in a wood.

~

In May 1872 Giuseppe Verdi received a letter:

Reggio Emilia
7 May 1872

Much honoured Signor Verdi,

The second of this month I went to Parma, drawn there by the sensation made by your opera *Aida*. So great was

my curiosity that one half-hour before the commence-
ment of the piece I was already in my place, No. 120. I
admired the *mise-en-scène*, I heard with pleasure the
excellent singers, and I did all in my power to let nothing escape me. At the end of the opera I asked myself if
I was satisfied, and the answer was 'No'. I started back
to Reggio and listened in the railway carriage to the
opinions given upon *Aida*. Nearly all agreed in considering it a work of the first order.

I was then seized with the idea of hearing it again,
and on the 4th I returned to Parma; I made unheard-of
efforts to get a reserved seat; as the crowd was enormous, I was obliged to throw away five lire to witness
the performance in any comfort.

I arrived at this decision about it: it is an opera in
which there is absolutely nothing which caused any
enthusiasm or excitement, and without the pomp of the
spectacle the public would not stand it to the end. When
it has filled the house two or three times, it will be
banished to the dust of the archives.

You can now, dear Signor Verdi, picture to yourself
my regret at having spent on two occasions thirty-two
lire; add to this the aggravating circumstances that I
depend on my family, and that this money troubles my
rest like a frightful spectre. I therefore frankly address
myself to you, in order that you may send me the
amount. The account is as follows:

	Lire
Railroad-going	2.60
” -returning	3.30
Theatre	8
Detestable supper at station	2
	15.9
Twice	31.80

Hoping that you will deliver me from the embarrassment, I salute you from my heart.

Bertani
(My address: Bertani Prospero,
Via San Domenico No. 5)

*Verdi at once wrote to his publisher, Giulio Ricordi, in
Milan, enclosing the letter with his own:*

You may well imagine that to protect the son of a
family from the spectres that pursue him, I will willingly pay the little bill which he sends me. I therefore
beg you to forward by one of your correspondents
to this M. Prospero Bertani the sum of 27 lire 80
centimes. It is not the amount he demands, but that in
addition I should be expected to pay for his supper,
certainly not! He might very well take his meals at
home.

It is understood that he will give you an acknowledgement, and further a short letter in reply, undertaking to hear my new operas no more, exposing himself no more to the menace of spectres, and sparing me further travelling expenses.

Arthur Pougin, Verdi, Histoire anecdotique, 1887

~

G. K. Chesterton on a present he had received:

A person of great generosity has given me for a Christmas present an enormous resplendent walking-stick — with silver bands, a shiny handle, and all sorts of things I had never heard of. Its splendour, indeed, creates a kind of problem. The walking-stick and I do not suit each other. The only question is, which shall give way? May it not reasonably be supposed that after a few days in my company the walking-stick may take on a more dingy, battered, and comfortable look? Or must I dress up to the walking-stick? In the fairy tales (on which I rely more and more) the touch of a wand can turn the Beast into a beautiful Prince. Perhaps the touch of this stick can turn the beast now under discussion into a beautiful dandy. Already I feel vaguely that I ought to have one neat kid glove with which to hold the stick. From this it is but a step to having good cuffs and shirt-links, and so the creeping paralysis of propriety may crawl up my arms and cover my whole person. In a year or so the stick may have transformed me wholly into its own image. Whether this will ever happen I do not know. What I do know is that if I walk down the streets with the stick at present most people mistake me for a tramp who has stolen a gentleman's walking-stick.

After earnest thought, prayer and meditation, I have come to the conclusion that it is my destiny in life to be a foil to the stick. I am only a background – a gloomy, a rugged background – against which the stick picks itself out in sparkling purity and distinctness. I suppose the strict grammatical definition of a walking-stick is a stick that can walk. I am sure this stick can walk by itself; I am merely a large, florid tassel attached to it. The people of Battersea will merely praise the stick as they see it passing along the street. Then, when their admiration of it is exhausted (if that be conceivable) they may add: 'And how artistic an idea to tie to this walking-stick an ill-dressed and unattract-ive human being, thus celebrating supremely in an image the victory of the inanimate over the animate.' I exist only to throw up the high light upon the lustrous stick. What matters it that I am abased so long as it is exalted? At any rate, this simple resolution to be a background to the stick is much less terrible than the other idea of living up to it.

~

Ask not what you can do for your country. Ask what's for lunch.

Orson Welles

~

Thomas Traherne lived from 1636 to 1674, but was unknown until the winter of 1896–7, when two manuscript volumes of his poems were discovered by chance in a street bookstall. His Centuries of Meditations, *which includes the following extraordinary passage, was first published in 1908:*

The corn was orient and immortal wheat, which never should be reaped, nor was ever sown. I thought it had stood from everlasting to everlasting. The dust and stones of the street were as precious as gold; the gates were at first the end of the world. The green trees when I saw them first through one of the gates transported and ravished me, their sweetness and unusual beauty made my heart to leap, and almost mad with ecstasy, they were such strange and wonderful things: The Men! O what venerable and reverend creatures did the aged seem! Immortal Cherubims! And young men glittering and sparkling Angels, and maids strange seraphic pieces of life and beauty! Boys and girls tumbling in the street, and playing, were moving jewels. I knew not that they were in their proper places. Eternity was manifest in the Light of the

Day; and something infinite behind everything appeared which talked with my expectation and moved my desire. The city seemed to stand in Eden, or to be built in Heaven. The streets were mine, the temple was mine, the people were mine, their clothes and gold and silver were mine, as much as their sparkling eyes, fair skins and ruddy faces. The skies were mine, and so were the sun and moon and stars, and all the World was mine; and I the only spectator and enjoyer of it. I knew no churlish proprieties, nor bounds, nor divisions; but all proprieties and divisions were mine; all treasures and the possessions of them. So that with much ado I was corrupted, and made to learn the dirty devices of this world. Which I now unlearn, and become, as it were, a little child again that I may enter into the Kingdom of God.

Traherne's work has been described as 'bafflingly simple' – which just about sums it up.

~

The Prince [of Wales] will be a spectator at an interfaith football match between Christian vicars and a team of imams in Berlin tomorrow. The fixture has already been named the Clash of Civilisations. The game will be staged as part of the Prince's tour and, if past form is anything to go by, he is likely to see the vicars thrashed. In a similar game last year, Islam beat Christianity 9–0. This time, though, the Christians – the line-up is likely to include a missionary, a Salvation Army major, a Swedish pastor and perhaps a Jesuit striker – should benefit from high-powered support.

The referee will be a rabbi and the linesmen will be two young men from the Berlin Jewish community.

The Times, 28 April 2009

The article concludes:

Finding a day for the fixture has always been complicated since the imams are busy on Fridays, the rabbis are otherwise engaged on Saturdays, and the Christian clerics are fully employed on Sundays. The timetable of the Prince of Wales has ensured a midweek game.

~

From my friend Marcia Carter comes the following passage from one of Martha Gellhorn's letters to Ernest Hemingway. It is dated 28 June 1943:

I wish we could stop it all now, the prestige, the possessions, the position, the knowledge, the victory: and that

173

we could by a miracle return together under the arch at Milan, with you so brash in your motor cycle side car and I, badly dressed, fierce, loving, standing in the street waiting for your picture to be taken. My God, how I wish it. I would give every single thing there now is to be young and poor with you. As poor as there was to be, and the days hard but always with that shine on them that came of not being sure, of hoping, of believing in fact in just the things we now so richly have.

~

I cannot resist this sonnet by Edna St Vincent Millay, brought to my attention by Michael Birkett:

Not in a silver casket cool with pearls
Or rich with red corundum or with blue,
Locked, and the key withheld, as other girls
Have given their loves, I give my love to you;
Not in a lovers'-knot, not in a ring
Worked in such fashion, and the legend plain—
Semper fidelis, where a secret spring
Kennels a drop of mischief for the brain:
Love in the open hand, no thing but that,
Ungemmed, unhidden, wishing not to hurt,
As one should bring you cowslips in a hat
Swung from the hand, or apples in her skirt,

I bring you, calling out as children do:
'Look what I have!—And these are all for you.'

~

We passed over the red roofs of Calicut, where Vasco da Gama made his first Indian landfall. Along here, in 1789, Tipu Sultan had engaged the British in a famous campaign that demonstrated how mobile, fast-moving guerrilla forces will always outflank a static army commanded by dull, conservative generals. Tipu, operating from a series of fortified hill-top *droogs*, ran rings around the British as they ponderously mounted the Ghats with their armaments – each cannon pushed by an elephant, while scores of men and oxen hauled on drag-ropes – and a stupefying amount of personal baggage. A typical captain went into battle with a large bed, several chairs, a folding table, two pairs of candle shades, twenty-four linen suits, several dozen bottles of wine, brandy and gin, tea, sugar and biscuits, a hamper of live poultry, a milch goat, seven trunks containing cooking utensils, cutlery, crystal and table linen, and a palanquin. The palanquin coolies were followed by a head boy, a lesser boy, a cook, an ostler, a grass-cutter and two bullock drivers for the four baggage bullocks.

Alexander Frater, *Chasing the Monsoon*

I have always enjoyed wakes: my father had a wonderful one, all his oldest and dearest friends carousing in the bar car of the train returning them to London after his funeral at Belvoir. So I'm particularly grateful to my stepson Roland for introducing me to this poem by John Fletcher (1579–1625):

The Dead Host's Welcome

'Tis late and cold; stir up the fires;
Sit close, and draw the table nigher;
Be merry, and drink wine that's old,
A hearty medicine 'gainst a cold.
Your beds of wanton down the best,
Where you shall tumble to your rest;
I could wish you wenches too,
But I am dead, and cannot do.
Call for the best the house may ring,
Sack, white, and claret let them bring,
And drink apace, while breath you have;
You'll find but cold drink in the grave.
Plover, partridge, for your dinner,
And a capon for the sinner,
You shall find ready when you're up,
And your horse shall have his sup:
Welcome, welcome, shall fly round.
And I shall smile, though under ground.

I suppose we tend to think of Fletcher – when we think of him at all – in connection with his collaborator Francis Beaumont. The two wrote plays together for nearly ten years, and – according to John Aubrey – lived together too, in Bankside, sharing their clothes and 'having one wench in the house between them'. But Beaumont married in 1613, and Fletcher joined the theatrical company of the King's Men, where he collaborated with Shakespeare on Henry VIII *– probably writing a good deal of it.*

~

I am reading, with total fascination, The Rational Optimist: How Prosperity Evolves *by Matt Ridley. Here is one memorable passage:*

The behaviour of Hongwu, the first of the Ming emperors, is an object lesson in how to stifle the economy: forbid all trade and travel without government permission; force merchants to register an inventory of their goods once a month; order peasants to grow for their own consumption and not for the market; and allow inflation to devalue the paper currency, 10,000-fold. His son Yong-Le added some more items to the list: move the capital at vast expense; maintain a gigantic army; invade Vietnam unsuccessfully; put your favourite eunuch in charge of a nationalised fleet of monstrous

ships with 27,000 passengers, five astrologers and a
giraffe, then in a fit of pique at the failure of this mission
to make a profit, ban everybody else from building ships
or trading abroad.

~

*Hugh Latimer (1487–1555) was Bishop of Worcester before
the Reformation, and later Church of England chaplain to
King Edward VI. He was burnt at the stake by Bloody Mary.
Here is an extract from one of his Christmas sermons:*

To show themselves obedient, came Joseph and Mary
unto Bethlehem; a long journey, and poor folks, and
peradventure on foot; for we read of no great horses that
she had, as our great ladies have nowadays; for truly she
had no such jolly gear . . .

Well, she was great with child, and was now come to
Bethlehem, where they could get never a lodging in no
inn, and so were compelled to lie in a stable; and there
Mary, the mother of Christ, brought forth that blessed
child . . . and there 'she wrapped Him in swaddling
clothes and laid Him in a manger, because there was no
room for them at the inn.' For the innkeepers took only
those who were able to pay for their good cheer; they
would not meddle with such beggarly folk as Joseph and
Mary his wife were . . .

But I warrant you, there was many a jolly damsel at that time in Bethlehem, yet amongst them all there was not one found that would humble herself so much as once to go and see poor Mary in the stable, and to comfort her. No, no; they were too fine to take so much pains, I warrant you, they had bracelets and vardingales; like as there be many nowadays amongst us, which study nothing else but how they may desire fine raiment; and in the mean season they suffer poor Mary to lie in the stable . . .

But what was her swaddling-clothes wherein she laid the King of heaven and earth? No doubt it was poor gear; peradventure it was her kercher which she took from her head, or such like gear; for I think Mary had not much fine linen; she was not trimmed up as our women be nowadays; for in the old time women were content with honest and single garments. Now they have found out these round-a-bouts; they were not invented then; the devil was not so cunning to make such gear, he found it out afterward.

Here is a question to be moved. Who fetched water to wash the child after it was born into the world, and who made a fire? It is like that Joseph did such things; for, as I told you before, those fine damsels thought it scorn to do any such thing unto Mary.

But, I pray you, to whom was the Nativity of Christ first opened? To the bishops, or great lords which were at that time at Bethlehem? Or to those jolly damsels with their vardingales, with their round-a-bouts, or with their bracelets? No, no; they had so many lets to trim and dress themselves, that they could have no time to hear of the Nativity of Christ.

But his nativity was narrated first to the shepherds . . .

~

In July 1949, at the end of the Eton summer half, the biology master Mr Gaddum — whom I well remember, since he taught me too — wrote a report on the work of one of his pupils, a certain John Gurdon:

It has been a disastrous half. His work has been far from satisfactory. His prepared stuff has been badly learnt, and several of his test pieces have been torn over [rejected]; one of such pieces of prepared work scored 2 marks out of a possible 50. His other work has been equally bad, and several times he has been in trouble because he will not listen, but will insist on doing his work in his own way. I believe he has ideas about becoming a Scientist; on his present showing this is quite ridiculous: if he can't learn simple Biological facts he would have no chance of doing the work of a specialist, and it would be sheer waste of time, both on his part and of those who have to teach him.

His marks were 231/550, place 15/15, 17/18, 18/18.

Just sixty-three years later in 2012, Sir John Gurdon won the Nobel Prize for Biology.

~

Sir George Sitwell writes to his son Osbert, soon after the beginning of the First World War:

14 December, 1914

My dearest Osbert,

As I fear a line sent to Chelsea Barracks may not reach you before you leave tomorrow, I write to you care of your regiment, B.E.F. [British Expeditionary Force] so that you may find a letter waiting for you when you arrive in the trenches. But I had wanted if possible to give you a word of advice before you left. Though you will not, of course, have to encounter anywhere abroad the same weight of gunfire that your mother and I had to face here* – it has been my contention for many years that there were no guns in the world to compare for weight and range with the great German naval guns, and that our own do not come anywhere near them – yet my experience may be useful to you. Directly you hear the first shell, retire, as I did, to the undercroft, and remain there quietly until all firing has ceased. Even then, a bombardment, especially as one grows older, is a strain upon the nervous system – but the best remedy for that, as always, is to keep warm and have plenty of plain, nourishing food at frequent but regular intervals. And, of course, plenty of rest. I find a nap in the afternoon most helpful, if not unduly prolonged, and I advise you to try it whenever possible.

* German guns had recently bombarded Scarborough.

~

On 24 August 1897 A. C. Benson dined with the Gladstones at Hawarden. Mr Gladstone was 87, she 85. Benson's biographer David Newsome writes:

As Arthur got up to leave, he was puzzled to pass a desk with an inkstand, against which was leaning a card with LUMBAGO written on it – nothing else. He enquired delicately what it meant. Mary Drew (Gladstone's daughter) laughed: 'It's one of the words my mother forgets. She is suffering from lumbago for the first time in her life, but can't remember the word.'

~

To Mrs Edward Austin Abbey, who regularly supplied him with eggs:

34 De Vere Gardens W.
Nov. 1, 1894

Dear Mrs Abbey,

We are very unhappy at the non-arrival of our eggs and are full of delicacy, at the same time, as to inquiring about them. Is the egg crop failing? Have the animals struck? Are we and they all victims of agricultural depression? I fear it, and if the disaster is at last upon us, won't you very kindly let me know the worst. I have been wanting yet fearing to write to you. Today at last I seem to find courage just to twitch the hem of your garment. I seem also to myself to have divined that you most naturally can't any longer be bothered by the bugbear of my breakfasts. It would indeed break down the patience of the angels. Nevertheless, a still, small hope does flicker in my breast. May we at any rate have news? News would be good, but eggs would be better. I shall hope for the best, but, after our tragic sob, I shall completely enter into the worst. With love to the master,

Yours, Mrs Abbey, in affectionate suspense,
Henry James

*John Spurling sent me the following extract from a letter from his
great-uncle Sir Edmund Gibson KCIE (1886–1974). He was at
the time Political Agent for the Kathiawar princely states.*

January 22, 1928

Last week I camped at a place called Khirana, an isolated
and insignificant village surmounted by a dilapidated
fort in which the ruler lives. His total revenues amount
to between £2,000 and £3,000 per annum. He does his
best for his state but is despondent and discontented. In
the past he had a glimpse of Paradise and is now a prey
to regret that he can never enter it again. His Paradise
was Bexhill where he spent two years, 1912 and 1913. I
gather that he moved in the more select tradesmen circles
and was much lionised. He showed me a picture of
himself in the *Bexhill Chronicle* and various trophies he
had won there. Tennis, badminton and roller skating
were his principal diversions. He is a well-intentioned
man and it is sad to see him brooding over a past that can
never return and comparing the dreary present with the
glorious life of Bexhill. He says that he does not let
himself dwell on the delights of those days but the
remembrances will recur, however much he tries to
banish them. A pathetic figure.

~

I am old. Nothing interests me now.
Moreover, I am not very intelligent,
And my ideas have travelled no further
Than my feet. You ask me
What is the greatest happiness on earth?
It is to hear a young girl
Singing along the road
After she has asked you the way.

                    Wang Wei (13th century)

~

The 2017 Cracker *opened with an account by my friend Ben
Macintyre of the only known occasion when Hitler is believed
to have played cricket, and the suggestions he made for the
improvement of the game. This has called forth from my friend
Peter Stormonth Darling the following passage from* The
Life of Golden Miller, *by Basil Briscoe, published in 1940:*

Sport is what every man, whether he be a peer or a
humble working man, should always have at heart. It has
been the backbone of this country and has had as many
struggles. The really true sportsman knows how to lose,
and also how to treat his fellow companions. If the
German people had been allowed to know that there was
comradeship between all well-wishers of human life,
and if those sporting instincts, which undoubtedly they

have at heart, had been allowed to have been developed by their dictators, the world might never have been placed in the position which it is in today. Really true sportsmen try to help their fellow folk, but I am afraid the German people, on account of their leaders, have not been brought up in this faith; had they been, they would have helped the many small countries which lay on their boundaries instead of invading them and using brute force. The school bully is all smiles when he has everything his way, but when things go against him he weakens quickly. Had Hitler been a sportsman, had he ever attended race meetings, hunted, played cricket, or entered into any of the fields of sport, he would not have plunged the whole world into the state in which we find it today. Sportsmen will realise that the Führer could not have had any of these sporting instincts in him.

Much the same thought occurred to Wodehouse:

I attribute the insane arrogance of the later Roman Emperors almost entirely to the fact that, never having played golf, they never knew that strangely chastening humility which is engendered by a topped chip-shot.

And a final postscript, once again from Ben Macintyre. On 24 February 2018 he wrote in The Times *of how Harold*

Wilson, when a member of Clement Attlee's cabinet, 'played cricket with Soviet officials near the Moskva river and boasted that he was the only batsman ever to be dropped at square leg by a member of the NKVD'.

∼

'The priests would tell you to pray that God's will be done.'

'I'd want to know what his will was before I prayed anything like that,' she said.

Graham Greene, *A Burnt-Out Case*

∼

I shall make it simple so you will understand.
Making it simple will make it clear for me.
When you have read it, take me by the hand
As children do, loving simplicity.

This is the simple poem I have made.
Tell me you understand. But when you do
Don't ask me in return if I have said
All that I meant, or whether it is true.

Anthony Thwaite, 'Simple Poem'

Experience is a good teacher, but her fees are very high.

Dean W. R. Inge

When I was just thirteen I met Dean Inge at breakfast. He was perfectly charming, and when he started talking about old age I plucked up courage and asked him what was the earliest thing he could remember. He took the question very seriously and was quite a long time replying; but when he did, it was worth it.

'I think,' he said, 'as a small boy, my first clear recollection is that of the outbreak of the American Civil War.'

He was in fact born in 1860, so his memory was perhaps a little at fault. But I am quite sure of his words.

~

Let the surgeon take care to regulate the whole regimen of the patient's life for joy and happiness, allowing his relatives and special friends to cheer him, and by having someone tell him jokes . . . Keep up the spirits of your patient with the music of the viol and the psaltery, by forging letters telling of the deaths of his enemies, or, if he be religious, by informing him that he has been made a bishop.

More surgeons know how to cause suppuration than how to treat a wound.

Henri de Mondeville, *Treatise on Surgery*, 1312

~

Since we parted, yestereve
I do love thee, love, believe,
Twelve times dearer, twelve hours longer,
One dream deeper, one night stronger,
One sun surer – thus much more
Than I loved thee, love, before.

Edward Robert Bulwer-Lytton

2019

2019: The Unfinished Christmas Cracker

John Julius would put together his annual *Cracker* over one weekend in February or March. He would leaf through the last two or three of his leather-bound commonplace books (he filled fourteen in all) in which every entry was inscribed by hand. From these he chose twenty-four pieces and typed them up, along with those felicitous introductions and explanations which, like all his writing, perfectly reflect the sound of his voice.

Having printed them off, he would lay the pages out on the bed. Since most people devoured the *Cracker* at a sitting the moment it arrived, a lot of trouble was taken to place the texts in a satisfying order. He would move them around until he had the balance right, then gather them into a pile for Mollie to read. Even as late as proof stage the order might change, if he felt that something in the sequence had failed to settle down.

John Julius corrected the proofs of the forty-ninth *Christmas Cracker* from his hospital bed, shortly before he died in June 2018. We thought it was the last; yet, a few months later, Mollie found that he had already chosen half the pieces for the fiftieth *Cracker* which would have appeared in 2019.

Incomplete as it is, the 2019 *Cracker* is a superb collection. It includes a medieval character sketch, an apology from *The Times*, a ticker-tape misprint, two frozen corpses, recollections of Catholic boarding schools for girls (not his, I hasten to add) and a sparkling handful of paraprosdokians. His reading was broad by any standards but, like all great collectors, his eyes were always open for the next treasure. What pleasure that keen anticipation, ever ready to pounce, must have brought to everything he read.

Artemis Cooper
July 2019

A commonplace book contains many nations in garrison, whence the owner may draw out an army into the field on competent warning.

Thomas Fuller, *The Holy and the Profane State*

~

Of the composer Charles Gounod:

His striking head was framed in a black beard. His fiery eyes shone with liveliness and spirit, his broad, high forehead revealed the depth and thought of a man of genius; but besides these attractive qualities, his marvellously expressive and intensely vital face was above all suffused with a feeling of such charm, such good will, that one was captivated, persuaded by a sense of understanding as strong as it was immediate.

Even as a novice in the world of the theatre, where charm is the stock in trade, he triumphed. 'I met a Mr Gounod,' writes Edmund Got the great comic actor, 'former Prix de Rome, a philandering monk, so they say,

and as talented musically as he is exuberant and shame-
lessly pushy as a man. He actually kissed me on both
cheeks the first time I ever met him! His opera [*Sapho*]
which was given a few days ago, was received creditably;
less so, however, than one would have expected from
hearing the score sung and played by him at the piano,
with no voice – but what charm!'

Voice or no voice, the charm was to endure into old
age – along with the weakness for kissing – as we know
from a description of him at seventy:

'Gounod spent all day Wednesday and Thursday
morning with us,' wrote Henri Meilhac, one of Bizet's
librettists for *Carmen*. 'Never in my life have I been
kissed so often in so short a time. He brought a M.
Dalicot and Mme Dalicot with him. M. Dalicot kisses
even more than Gounod, but he kisses only Gounod,
flinging himself at the master from time to time and kissing him three or four times in succession. The master
does not appear surprised by this; he returns the kisses
and says "my son". Mme Dalicot he calls "my daughter", so that the relationship is not really very clear.
Gounod sat down at the piano and played all Wednesday
evening; because of that I forgave him his kissing bouts.'

Mina Curtiss, *Bizet and His World*

~

Two letters to The Times, *the first dated Christmas Eve 2012:*

Sir,

Captain Scott and his two companions do not quite lie where they died (letter, Dec. 21); during the last 100 years they have moved on. Their last camp was on the Ross Ice Shelf, afloat on the Ross Sea, where the ice is approximately 110 m thick. The bodies are moving slowly towards the ice front, while being buried ever deeper as snow accumulates. They have already travelled about 60 km and will reach the sea, 350 km away, in the year 2470, about 560 years after their journey began.

John White
Chipstead, Surrey

The second appeared on 26 April 2014 and ran as follows:

Sir,

A Swansea scientist (report, Apr. 23) says that 'sloths take thirty days to digest a leaf and go to the bathroom once a week'. This takes euphemism to a new level.

Andrew Dakyns
Eastbourne

Ticker-tacker, ticker-tacker. A tape machine jerked into life in the office . . . Major Denzil Batchelor had come in early to finish his report on the Norway debate. The Intelligence Officer thrust himself from his chair to pick up a page that had fallen to the floor, and read: 'Hotler's troops have overrun Luxembourg; Dutch and Belgian cabinets appeal to France; Hotler proclaims fall of Belgium and Holland; Hotler says he will crush Britain; Hotler says . . .' The machine paused. Then out rolled another sheet. 'Correction for Hotler: read Hitler and the meaning will immediately become apparent.'

Nicholas Shakespeare, Six Minutes in May

~

Within my soul are some mean gardens found,
Where droopèd flowers are, and unsung melodies
And all companioning of piteous things;
But in the midst is one high-terraced ground
Where level lawns sweep through the stately trees
And the great peacocks walk like painted kings.

Lord Alfred Douglas, The City of the Soul

~

Terms and Conditions *is a study by Ysenda Maxtone Graham of girls' boarding schools in England between the 1930s and the 1970s, and is one of the funniest books I have ever read. Here are a few extracts:*

Wings was in Charlton Park in Wiltshire, mullioned up to the eaves, with plentiful turrets. The headmistress was out of her depth, and a heavy drinker. 'Every Saturday night we had ballroom dancing in the great marble hall,' said Caroline (Cranbrook), 'and the headmistress sat drumming her fingers, with a cigarette hanging out of her mouth and a glass of crême de menthe. We had to dance with her father, who'd been wounded as a sapper in the First World War; either he had his "arms" on, with black gloves, or he couldn't be bothered to put them on and we just had to dance with the stumps.' Oddly enough, the school sport was rugby: the headmistress seemed to enjoy this. 'Jump on me, girls, jump on me!' she would say . . .

Snobbery was rampant, particularly in the Roman Catholic schools. The headmistress of St Mary's Ascot from 1956 to 1976 was Mother Bridget. Mother Bridget taught Latin to the juniors, and she kicked off the first Latin lesson of the new 11-year-olds in 1976 with this ice-breaker: 'Now hands up any of you whose house is open to the public.' 'Quite a few hands did go up,' remembers Maggie Fergusson, 'and this started a chat about a few of the girls' stately homes, before we started doing any Latin.'

Old Reverend Mother Gregory, who had herself been educated at Cambridge in the 1930s, was supposed to prepare a handful of 1970s girls for the Oxbridge General Paper. When it trickled out to some parents that she had said, 'What you have to realise, girls, is that the lower classes don't speak to each other, they grunt', it was decided that enough was enough . . .

This, Maggie Fergusson told me, was how the Reverend Mother, Mother Isabel, addressed the girls when it became known that a man had escaped from Broadmoor psychiatric hospital, ten miles away: 'Now girls, should you meet this gentleman on your way back through the woods from the junior house, this is what you should do. If he initiates a conversation, you should simply join in and agree with him. So if he says, "I am the Queen of Sheba", you should reply, "yes, you are the Queen of Sheba." But if he doesn't initiate a conversation, you should say something perfectly natural to him, such as "Are you a caddy from the *goff* course?"'

The music mistress at St Helen's, Northwood in the early 1950s went on a Hellenic cruise. On board she made friends with one of the lecturers and on her return invited him to come and give a lecture to the school. A day or two after the lecture the headmistress, Miss Mackenzie, announced to the girls: 'Next term Miss Wilmot will be known as Lady Shelley.'

When I asked a group of 1960s Hatherop Castle girls whether their school had a lab in those days, they gave me a blank look. 'A laboratory', I expanded, hoping to jog their memories. 'Oh, *that* kind of lab,' one of them said. 'I thought you meant a Labrador.'

~

A particularly promising book beginning is that of Desmond Seward's The Demon's Brood*:*

In 999, a Plantagenet forebear, Count Fulk the Black of Anjou, had his young wife, Elisabeth of Vendôme, burned alive in her wedding dress in the marketplace at his capital of Angers, in front of the cathedral, after catching her *in flagrante* with a goatherd.

~

Diary entry by the Rev. John Wesley:

On May 5 I preached at St Aldate's to a very numerous congregation. So enlarged was my heart to declare the Word of God to all that were oppressed by the devil that I was not in the least surprised when I was afterwards told: Sir, you must preach here no more.

My friend Brian Young told me some years ago that such a sentence with a surprise ending is called a paraprosdokian. Other examples are Dorothy Parker's:

If all the girls who attended the Yale prom were laid end to end, I wouldn't be a bit surprised.

Or Groucho Marx's:

I've had a perfectly wonderful evening, but this wasn't it.

Or Ogden Nash's:

If at first you don't succeed, the hell with it.

Or Alice Roosevelt Longworth's:

If you can't think of anything nice and kind to say about anyone – why, do come and sit beside me.

~

The Times' *third leader of 18 June 2015:*

We would like to acknowledge that our words, in a leading article in 1856 in which we wrote that Verdi's opera *La Traviata* was 'the impersonation of all that is most foul and hideous in human nature', could have been misconstrued. Many readers, in fact, gained the impression that we did not appreciate Verdi's work. Such an impression was perhaps emphasised when we went on to say that this was an opera which 'should never have been exhibited on any stage, in the presence of decent womanhood'.

It is important to stress that the reasoning behind this judgement was sound. The objection *The Times* was making, perhaps in unnecessarily florid terms, was not that the opera was a contribution to moral turpitude. When we declared that it was 'as unnecessary as it would be disgusting to enter here into minute particulars', the minute particulars in question were not of a sexual kind, even though the libretto does describe the journey of a courtesan through polite society.

Verdi's work contains the depiction of consumption, a fatal illness whose portrayal on the stage could be counted on to cause untold distress to audiences. It was the threat to public health that we found to be 'repulsive', rather than the threat to public morals. We would also like to clarify that, in so far as our leading article was slightly outraged by the depiction of fruity affairs, it was inspired by the fear that menfolk in the audience might be inclined to copy what was called 'an exhibition of harlotry' and take up with prostitutes. We now accept that the gentlemen of Britain are nothing like as weak as this.

Now that *La Traviata* is the most popular work in the operatic canon, and the subject of a new documentary about its run-in with this newspaper, we unreservedly apologise for any offence caused. *The Times* regrets the error.

~

The new edition, published in 2007, of the Oxford Junior Dictionary *has omitted a number of words which it considers to be no longer relevant to twenty-first-century childhood. The list includes the following:*

Acorn, adder, ash, beech, bluebell, buttercup, catkin, conker, cowslip, cygnet, dandelion, fern, hazel, heather, heron, ivy, kingfisher, lark, mistletoe, nectar, newt, otter, pasture and willow.

The words introduced for the first time now include:

Attachment, block-graph, blog, broadband, bullet-point, celebrity, chatroom committee, cut-and-paste, MP3 player and voicemail.

One of the best medieval character sketches I know: that of Roger, Archbishop of Reggio di Calabria in the late twelfth century, as described by Hugo Falcandus:

Already on the brink of old age, he was tall and so excessively thin that he appeared to be eaten away from the inside. His voice was weak as a whistle. His face, and indeed his whole body, was pale and yet somehow tinged with blackness, making him look more like a corpse than a man; and his external aspect well indicated the character within. He counted no labour difficult if there were hope of a gain therefrom; and he would willingly endure hunger and thirst beyond the limits of human tolerance in order to save money. Never happy at his own table, he was never sad at those of others, and would frequently spend whole days without food, waiting to be invited to dinner.

~

I get into bed, turn out the light, say 'bugger the lot of them' and go to sleep.

Winston Churchill

Acknowledgements

Grateful acknowledgement is given to the following for permission to reproduce copyright material: Letter from Carlo Ardito to *The Times* reprinted by kind permission of Laurence Fitch Ltd. Article on the dawn chorus first published in *The Times*, reproduced by kind permission of Simon Barnes. Extract from *D-Day: The Battle for Normandy* by Antony Beevor (Viking, 2009), reproduced courtesy of the author. 'On a Sundial' from *Sonnets and Verses* by Hilaire Belloc reprinted by permission of Peters Fraser & Dunlop (www.petersfraserdunlop. com) on behalf of the Estate of Hilaire Belloc. Extract from 'Huxley Hall' from John Betjeman, *Collected Poems*, reprinted courtesy of John Murray (Publishers). Extract from *A Short History of Nearly Everything* by Bill Bryson published by Black Swan. Reproduced by permission of The Random House Group Ltd. © 2016. Extract from the index to *The Violent Effigy* by John Carey, reproduced by permission of Faber & Faber Ltd. Extract from Adrian Carton De Wiart, *Happy Odyssey*, published by Pen & Sword Military (2011). Quotes reproduced from the speeches, works and writings of Winston S. Churchill: reproduced with permission of Curtis Brown, London on behalf of The Estate of Winston S. Churchill. © The Estate of Winston S. Churchill. 'Forgetfulness' from *Questions About Angels* by Billy Collins © 1995. Reprinted by permission of the University of Pittsburgh Press. Extract from Noel Coward's autobiography, © NC Aventales as successor to the Estate of Noel Coward, 2004, *Future Indefinite*, Methuen Drama, an imprint of Bloomsbury Publishing Plc. 'When I Have Fears, as Keats Had Fears' by Noel Coward, © NC Aventales as successor to the Estate of Noel Coward, 2011, *The Complete Verse of Noel Coward*, Methuen Drama, an imprint of Bloomsbury Publishing Plc. Extract *from Bizet and His World* by Mina Curtiss published by Secker & Warburg. Reproduced by permission of The Random House Group Ltd. © 1959. 'Alternative Endings to an Unwritten Ballad' by Paul Dehn reproduced courtesy of Berlin Associates Ltd. Extract from David Hare, *Racing Demon* (Faber & Faber, 2001), reproduced by permission of Casarotto Ramsay & Associates. 'Merry Christmas, Happy New Year' copyright © 1958 by Phyllis McGinley. First published by Viking Press/Secker & Warburg. Reprinted by permission of Curtis Brown, Ltd. 'On Being Seventy' copyright © 1978 by Phyllis McGinley. Reprinted by permission of Curtis Brown, Ltd. 'The Life That I Have' by Leo Marks reproduced with permission of Souvenir Press. Extracts from *Terms and Conditions* by Ysenda Maxtone Graham (Slightly Foxed, 2016) reprinted courtesy of the author. 'This Poem' by Elma Mitchell © The Estate of Harry Chambers for the Estate of Elma Mitchell, from Elma Mitchell, *People Etcetera* (Peterloo Poets, 1987). Answer to the question 'Is Hell exothermic or endothermic?' reproduced courtesy of Michael Pakenham. Extract from Matt Ridley, *The Rational Optimist* reprinted by permission of HarperCollins Publishers Ltd © Matt Ridley 2010. 'Adam' © Siegfried Sassoon reproduced by kind permission of the Estate of George Sassoon. Extract from Stanley R. Sims, 'Sir Wilfred Grenfell: An Athletic Missionary', *BMJ*, 305, 19–26 December 1992, p.525, reproduced by kind permission of *BMJ*. 'Limerick', from *The Collected Poems of Dylan Thomas: The Centenary Edition* (Weidenfeld & Nicolson, 2014), © The Dylan Thomas Trust, reproduced with permission of David Higham Associates. 'Simple Poem' by Anthony Thwaite from Anthony Thwaite, *Selected Poems* (Enitharmon Editions, 1997), reproduced with permission of Enitharmon Editions. Extract from *Paul Tortelier: A Self-Portrait – In Conversation with David Blum* published by Heinemann (1984). 'Not in a Silver Casket Cool With Pearls' by Edna St Vincent Millay reprinted courtesy of Holly Peppe, Literary Executor, The Millay Society (millay.org). 'Le Jaseroque' by Frank L. Warrin, first printed in the *New Yorker*, 10 January 1931. Letter from Philip Ziegler to John Julius Norwich reprinted with kind permission of Philip Ziegler.

Every reasonable effort has been made to trace copyright holders, but if there are any errors or omissions, John Murray will be pleased to insert the appropriate acknowledgement in any subsequent printings or editions.

Index

Page numbers in italic indicate a direct quotation from cited author or other source.

Abbey, Mrs Edward
Austin, 183
Addison, Joseph,
124–5
Alington, C. A., 128
Allen, Cardinal
William, 28
Ardito, Carlo, *80*
Asquith, Raymond, 57
Attlee, Clement, 144
Aubrey, John, 177
Auden, W. H., 139
Auto Cor Strike a
Light, 106

Baden-Powell, (Sir)
Robert, 1st Baron, 47
Balfour, Arthur James,
57
Balfour, Lady Frances,
129
Barnes, Simon, *162–3*
Bartlett, Bob, 109
Batchelor, Major
Denzil, 198
Beament, Sir James,
105–7
Beaumont, Francis,
177
Beckford, William,
41–2
Beecham, Sir Thomas,
59

Beevor, Sir Antony, 77,
165
Belloc, Hilaire, 159,
160
Benchley, Robert, 151
Bennet, Dr
Christopher, 50
Benson, A. C., 182
Beresford, Admiral
Lord Charles, 116
Beresford, Lord
Delaval, 115
Beresford, Lord
William, VC, 116
Berlin, Sir Isaiah, 38
Bertani, Prospero,
166–8
Betjeman, Sir John,
140, *157*
Betjeman, Penelope,
26
Bexhill, 184
bidets, 152
Birkett, Michael, 174
Blue-Beard, 81–4
Boatswain (Byron's
dog), 27
Boldini, Giovanni,
142
book beginnings,
100–1
Bowen, Charles, *69*
Bowra, Maurice, 26

Bradfield Women's
Institute, 134
Brandreth, Gyles,
151–2
Brindley, Rev. Brian
Frederick, 145–8
Briscoe, Basil, *185–6*
Brodie, Alec, 153–5
Browne, Sir Thomas,
21
Bryson, Bill, *126–8*
Buckland, William,
Dean of
Westminster, 66
Bulwer-Lytton *see*
Lytton
Burgess, Anthony,
101
Burkhart, Melvin, 114
Burne-Jones, Sir
Edward, 116
butterflies, 94–5
Byron, George Gordon,
6th Baron, 27

Carey, John, 43
Carroll, Lewis
(Charles Lutwidge
Dodgson), *11–13*;
'Jabberwocky':
translated, *21–4*
Carryl, Guy Wetmore,
81–4

208

Carter, Marcia, 173
Carton de Wiart,
    Lieutenant-General
    Sir Adrian, VC,
    135–7
Casati, Marchesa
    Luisa, 142–3
Castiglione,
    Baldassare, 138
Cecil, Sir Robert, 101
Chaplin, Henry, 29
Charlemagne,
    Emperor of the
    West, 32–3
Charles, Prince of
    Wales, 77, 172–3
Charlton Park,
    Wiltshire, 199
Chekhov, Anton, 142
Chesterfield, Philip
    Dormer Stanhope,
    4th Earl of, 164
Chesterton, G. K.,
    169–70
Christmas, 45–7
Christmas Crackers:
    compilation and
    publication, 193
Churchill, Winston:
    on colour, 53; on
    painting, 52;
    presides at Cabinet
    meetings, 144; on
    retiring to bed,
    205
Clark, Catherine J., 80
cocktails, 68
Cole, G. D. H., 155–6
Collins, Billy, 140–1
Colvin, Howard, 85
commonplace books,
    1–3, 195
condoms, 117

Congreve, William,
    124
Cooper, Agnes, Lady
    (née Lady Agnes
    Duff), 90
Cooper, Sir Alfred,
    89–90
Cooper, Artemis, 131,
    193–4
Cooper, Lady Diana,
    x
Cooper, Jason, 117
Copenhagen
    (Wellington's
    horse), 27
Cork Examiner, 67
Coward, Noel, 53–5,
    133–4
Crewe, Quentin,
    65–6
cricket, 187
Cumberland, William
    Augustus, Duke of,
    16
Curtiss, Mina, 195–6

Dakyns, Andrew, 197
Dalicot, M. & Mme,
    196
Dante Alighieri, 28
Darley, George, 152
Darling, Peter
    Stormonth, 185
date palms, 39–40
daughters, 142
Dehn, Paul, 70–2
Dickens, Charles, 96
dictations, 57–8
diseases, 60–1
Disraeli, Benjamin,
    143–4
Douglas, Lord Alfred,
    198

Douglas-Home,
    William, 128
Drabble, Margaret,
    159
Drake, Julius, 142
Drew, Mary, 182
Dryden, John, 161–2
Dugdale, Lady
    Frances, 129
Dysart, Lionel
    Tollemache, 5th
    Earl of, 84

Edward VII, King, 90
Elisabeth of Vendôme,
    201
epitaphs, 19, 27, 38,
    56, 85, 158
Epstein, Jacob, 142–3
euphemisms, 197
Evans, Howard, 25
expenses, 75
Eyre, Richard, 158

Falcandus, Hugo, 205
Falloon, Shirley,
    105–7
Fergusson, Maggie,
    199–200
Fermor, Patrick Leigh,
    20, 30, 131–2,
    164–5
Fitzgerald, Lord
    Edward, 74–5
Flanders, Judith, 116
Fletcher, John, 176–7
football, 172–3
Ford, Thomas, 126
forgetfulness, 140–1
Fraser, Jenny, 60
Frater, Alexander, 175
Fulk the Black, Count
    of Anjou, 201

Fuller, Buckminster, 55–6
Fuller, Thomas, *195*

Gaddum, Mr (Eton biology teacher), *180*
Gandhi, Mohandas Karamchand (Mahatma), 128
Gardiner, Isabella, 102
Gaskell, Helen Mary, 116
Gellhorn, Martha, *173–4*
George II, King: funeral, 16–17
George III, King, 84
Gibbon, Edward, *10–11, 40–1*, 41–2
Gibson, Sir Edmund, *184*
Gilbert, Sir John, *101–2*
girls' boarding schools, 199–201
Gladstone, Mrs, 182
Gladstone, William Ewart, 143–4, 182
Goldwyn, Sam, *160*
golf, 186
Goodhart-Rendel, H. S., 140
Gordian, Roman Emperor, 40–1
Got, Edmund, 195
Gounod, Charles, 195–6
Greene, Graham, *187*
Greenfield, Mrs (of Brighton), *99–100*
Grenfell, Sir Wilfred, 109–10

Grigson, Geoffrey, 13
Grimond, Jo, 128
Gurdon, Sir John, 180–1
Guthrie, Bob, 118

Hambro, Ruth, 108
Hammerstein-Equord, General Freiherr Kurt von, *131*
Hare, Sir David, *158*
Harton, Rev. F. P., *26*
Haydon, Benjamin Robert, *17, 44*
Head, Antony, 25
hedgehogs, 130
Hell, 102–5
Hemingway, Ernest, 173–4
Herodotus, *44*
Herrick, Robert, *92–3*
Highway Code: Japan, 91
History of World Architecture (John Julius Norwich), 55
Hitler, Adolf, 185–6
Hobsbawm, Eric, 149
Hobson, Anthony, 42
Hoby (London bootmaker), 132–3
Hodge, Patricia, 134
Holmes, Mr Justice, 137
holorhymes, 18–19
Hongwu, Ming Emperor, 177
Housman, A. E., *153*
Hugo, Victor, *18*

indexes, 43
Indians (North American), 78–80

Inge, W. R., Dean of St Paul's, *188*
IRA (Irish Republican Army), 148–9

James, Henry, *183*
Japan: Highway Code, 91
Jencks, Maggie (*née* Keswick), 91
Jenkins, Roy, *155*
Jerome, Jennie (Lady Randolph Churchill), *143–4*
Johnson, Samuel, *164*
Joseph, St, 178–9
Julius II, Pope, 102

Kelly, Linda, 72
Kipling, Rudyard, *51–2, 110–12*
Kuo Hsi, *21*

La Fontaine, Jean de, *59*
Lamb, Charles, *86*
Lancaster, Sir Osbert, 140
Lascelles, Sir Alan, 57
Laski, Harold J., 137
Latimer, Hugh, Bishop of Worcester, *178–80*
life forms: development, 126–8
limericks, 115, 145
Lincoln, USS, 113–14
Longford, Elizabeth, Countess of, *132–3*
Longworth, Alice Roosevelt, *202*
Louis XIV, King of France, 65–6
Lucretius, *161–2*

Luther, Martin, *119*
Lytton, Edward
    George Earle Lytton
    Bulwer-, 1st Baron,
    100
Lytton, Edward Robert
    Bulwer-, 1st Earl of,
    189

McGinley, Phyllis,
    45–7, 81
Machin, Ken, 106
Macintyre, Ben, 185–6
McLeod, Enid, 33
Macmillan, Harold,
    164–5
McPhee, John, 127
Magagula, Ephraem, 93
Marcellinus,
    Ammianus, *39–40*
Marks, Leo, *107*, 108
Martin, Kingsley, *144*
Marx, Groucho, *117*,
    202
Mary Queen of Scots,
    149
Mary, Virgin, 178–9
Mattingly, Garrett, *28*,
    161
Maxtone Graham,
    Ysenda, *199–201*
Medina Sidonia, Alonzo
    Pérez de Gusmàn,
    Duque de, *160–1*
Meilhac, Henri, 196
Mellon, Paul, *77–8*
memorials *see* epitaphs
memory, 140–1
Michelangelo
    Buonarroti, 102
Millay, Edna St
    Vincent, *174–5*
Mitchell, Elma, *159*

Mitford, Diana, 137
Mitford, Nancy, 137
mnemonics, 30–1
Mondeville, Henri de,
    189
Moore, Thomas, *8–9*,
    75
Motley, J. L., *29*
Muffett, Dr Thomas,
    50–1
Mulbarton, Norfolk:
    church of St Mary
    Magdalene, 38

Napoleon I
    (Bonaparte),
    Emperor of the
    French: possessions,
    76–7
Nash, Ogden, *202*
nativity (Christ's),
    178–80
Needham, Richard, *101*
Nerval, Gérard de, 48,
    49
Nevinson, H. W., *28*
New York University:
    applications, 96–8
Newcastle-under-
    Lyme, Thomas
    Pelham-Holles, 1st
    Duke of, 16
Newsome, David, *182*
nightingales, 162–3
nimgimmers, 89

operatic overtures,
    69–70
Otto, Count of
    Lomello, *32–3*
Otto III, Holy Roman
    Emperor, 32–3
Owen, Wilfred, *15*

*Oxford Junior
    Dictionary*, 204

painting, 52
Pakenham, Michael,
    104–5
palindromes, 10
palm trees, 39–40
parakeets, 101–2
paraprosdokians, 202
Parker, Dorothy, *202*
Parthenon, Athens,
    140
pennillion (Welsh
    improvised verse), 13
Pepys, Samuel, *31–2*
Pevsner, Sir Nikolaus,
    56
Philip II, King of
    Spain, 160
Philipps, Roland, 176
pig-sticking, 47–8
Pirosh, Robert, *124*
Pleshchev, Alexander,
    99
Pougin, Arthur, *169*
Priestley, J. B., *156*
puffins, 50–1

Ralegh, Sir Walter, *73*
Ravoon, Mrs (imaginary
    figure), 70–2
Reading Without Tears
    (Favell Lee
    Mortimer), *7–8*
revolving doors, 80
Ricordi, Giulio, 168
Ridley, Matthew,
    177–8
Roger, Archbishop of
    Reggio di Calabria,
    205
Rose, David, 28

Ross, Harold, 151
Rossini, Gioachino, 69–70
Ruskin, John, *59*, *139*

Sainsbury, Anya, 99
St Mary's Church, Paddington Green, 19
saints' relics, 157
salads, 67–8
Sassoon, Siegfried, *14*
Scarborough, 182
Scargill, Sarah, 38
Scott, Captain Robert Falcon, 197
sea, the, 152
Sealth (Seattle), Indian Chief, *78–80*
Seward, Desmond, *201*
Shakespeare, Nicholas, *198*
Shakespeare, William, 31–2
Shapiro, Virginia, 140
Shapur II, Persian King, 10–11
Sibelius, Jan, 53–5
Simon, John, 155–6
Sims, Stanley R., *109–10*
Sinclair-Loutit, Kenneth, 108
Sitwell, Sir George, *181–2*
Slade, Miss (Mahatma Gandhi's companion), 128
sloths, 197
Smith, John Alexander, *37*, 38
Smith, Sydney, *67–8*
Soames, Mary, 158

Southwell, Robert, *149–51*
sport, 172–3, 185–7
Spurling, John, 184
Squire, Sir J. C., *60–1*
Stark, Freya, *148*
sundials, 159–60
surgeons, 188–9
Sutcliffe, Tony, 85
Suvorin, Alexei, 142
Swallow, Charles, 158
swans, 50
Swaziland, 93
Szabo, Violette, 108–9

Taglioni, Marie, 99
Talleyrand, Charles Maurice de, *84*
Tan, Dr and Mrs (of Singapore), 105
tattoos, 116
Temple, Shirley, *70*
Thatcher, Margaret, 129–30
Thomas, Dylan, *145*
Thurber, James, 13, *14*
Thwaite, Ann, 155
Thwaite, Anthony, *187*
Tipu Sultan, 175
Tolstoy, Count Lev, 142
Topsell, Edward, *130*
Tortelier, Pau (Paul's daughter), 94–5
Tortelier, Paul, *94–5*
Traherne, Thomas, *171–2*
Troy, Trojans, 164–5

Turner, J. M. W., 59–60

Valdrati (Valdré), Vincenzo, 84–5
Verdi, Giuseppe: *Aida*, 166–8; *La Traviata*, 203–4
Vickers, Hugo, 135
Vilmorin, Louise de, 18

Wagner, Richard, 139
wakes, 176
walking-sticks, 169–70
Walpole, Horace, *16–17*
Wang Wei, *185*
Waterford, Henry de la Poer, 3rd Marquess of, 115
Waterloo, battle of (1815), 44–5, 132
Welles, Orson, *171*
Wellington, Arthur Wellesley, 1st Duke of, 44, 132–3
Wesley, John, *201*
White, Gilbert, *25*
White, John, *197*
Wilde, Oscar, 29
Wilder, Billy, 151–2
Wilder, Thornton, *81*
Wilkinson, Ellen, *144*
Wilson, Harold, 186–7
Wodehouse, P. G., *186*
women, 178–80

Yong-Le, 177
Young, Brian, 152

Ziegler, Philip, 57, *153–5*